Learning Pathways

Thank you to the staff and children in the schools that I have worked with and to friends and colleagues who have provided photographs to enable us to share the vision. Special thanks to Early Years Team Medway, Dimensions Foundation Nebraska, Ashbrow Centre Kirklees, Early Years Team Rochdale, Penhill Primary School Wiltshire.

© Claire Warden 2007
First published 2007

The rights of Claire Warden to be identified as the author of this work have been asserted in accordance with the Copyright Designs and Patents Act 1988.

Design & layout by Jan Vickers 2007

© Photography by Claire Warden & Niki Buchan 2007

ISBN 978-1-906116-05-7

If you would like in-service on this book, please contact Mindstretchers Ltd.

**Mindstretchers Ltd
The Warehouse
Rossie Place
Auchterarder
Perthshire
PH3 1AJ**

**Tel/Fax: 01764 664409
www.mindstretchers.co.uk**

Foreword

"The future is not some place we are going to, but one we are creating. The paths are not to be found, but made, and the activity of making them changes both the maker and the destination."

John Schaar

My pathway in education has taken me through all aspects of teaching and learning. Through working with parents and children in a home-based environment one quickly becomes aware of how important those early connections are and how we are co-educators with them in the process of educating their children. The path for many children takes a variety of different forms though the early years with some in full day care, nursery provision and others at home. In these environments children face a range of values and beliefs that should flow throughout their schooling. The transition into more formalised education should be smooth, with common threads running through relating to methodology and curriculum.

An educational pathway should be broad enough to allow children to move along their own learning path within a framework of opportunities that is set up to allow them to be successful, confident individuals who can contribute effectively in order to become a responsible citizen. It is this positive approach that is influencing curriculum change in Scotland at the moment. A curriculum for excellence is currently being developed and many practitioners hope that it will provide them with a broader pathway to allow them the flexibility and time to teach children in a way that ensures deeper learning and motivation.

This book explores some of the practical aspects of organising activity-based learning in the early years. To make the text accessible I have used the terms play, active learning and experiential learning to represent the same behaviour, that is, that children are actively involved in their own learning. The journey to excellence has to incorporate all the facets of a child's life since they are all connected. Children deserve rich, high quality environments.

I do hope you enjoy the book and feel able dip into it along your journey. If you would like to discuss any aspect of this approach then get in touch.

Contents

Foreword	3
Contents	5
Introduction	7
Creating the Ethos	11
Harmonisation to Create a Curriculum for Excellence	15
Organisation & Management	23
Time	24
Resources	27
Space	30
People	33
Planning for Play	35
Talking & Thinking Floorbooks ™	42
Consulting children in the planning process	
Assessment for Learning	45
Activity Zones	52
Role Play	53
Discovery Den	57
Learning in Outdoor Spaces	60
Materials Tray	65
Small World/Construction	68
Creating a Cohesive Approach	72
Appendix 1	
Meeting the Challenges of Shared Spaces	74
Case Study	76
Bibliography	79

Introduction

The Learning Path - Harmonisation of a Curriculum for 3-8 Year Olds

This book is designed to create an overview of the learning opportunities that can be created along a continuum of development from 3-8 years.

It is based on the following principles of good practice that are believed to be the key issues surrounding life long learning.

- People have a right to learn in positive environments that puts them at the centre of the learning process.

- People develop emotionally, intellectually, morally, physically, spiritually and socially, and at differing rates. All aspects of development are equally important and are interwoven.

- People have a right to learn with others who know them and are trying to understand the way they learn.

- People learn and retain information in different ways according to their brain physiology, learning style and preference.

- People retain information more effectively when they are interested and self motivated by the subject or method of teaching.

- People can be taught strategies that will help them to learn.

- People never stop learning.

- People learn at varying rates, and need time to assimilate and apply information if learning is to be effective.

We can gather a great deal from research and then apply it to our own practice, but at the core of effective teaching there has to be an internal, personal belief.
Before you start to explore this book, give yourself a moment to reflect on your own philosophy about how children learn. You may want to consider the following questions.

'Fascination and engagement leads to learning'

Children are:

- unique.
  So should they all be treated the same?

- individuals with their own way of learning.
  Do you know how they learn?

- already accomplished learners with existing frameworks of understanding.
  Do you know what they already know?

- energetic, active, curious and inquisitive.
  Are they being made to be passive?

- thinkers.
  Are they being consulted? Challenged?

- developing communication skills.
  Are they being allowed to use them?

- trying to be independent.
  Are you encouraging or suppressing this?

- developing their self esteem.
  Are they feeling good about being with you?

'Gravel tray construction area'

There is a great deal of evidence that children are challenged by the change of methods used when moving across environments they encounter between 3 and 8 years old.

There are a number of schools across Scotland who are responding to the growing band of evidence from sources such as HMI inspections and self evaluations that children learn through active involvement in the learning process. Rather than being a bolt on to the work programme in schools, the experiential approach can be integral so that children are given a balance of written, oral and practical experiences across a learning session at any point in the day.

One of the statements made in the Early Intervention in Literacy and Numeracy is that there is;

…'Widespread concern that there was too little play and opportunity for self-directed learning in the early stages of the primary school…'. Scottish Executive 2001.

It is surprising that a study carried out 19 years earlier by Cleave, Jowlett and Bate (1982) found very similar findings in a table that compared environments that children experience in the early years namely, primary school, nursery schools, playgroups, day centres and childminders. The research looked at the type of activities on offer in these environments, even down to waiting time. In the reverse order the percentage was 1 minute at a childminders, 3.9 minutes at day centres, 3.6 minutes at playgroups, 1.6 minutes in nursery classes and a staggering 9.3 minutes in the primary school. The time in the primary school was 32.4 % of time in sedentary tasks with active opportunities presented through a hall time. How much has changed? A great deal of information about the brain and how it learns is now available to practitioners and there are many primary schools who are developing early years practice from 3-8 years in light of research and clear evidence in terms of long term academic achievement.

In response to this, the book has been divided into chapters to make it easy to dip into. At the end of each section there are practical suggestions of opportunities and techniques to use.

- Creating the Ethos of the learning environment
- Curriculum for Excellence
- Organisation and Management -Time, resources, space, and people
- Planning for Play
- Talking & Thinking Floorbooks™ - Consulting children in the planning process
- Assessment within active learning
- Activity zones - Role play, Discovery Den, Learning in outdoor spaces, Materials Tray, Small World/Construction.
- Bibliography

The file that supports this book includes examples of practice e.g. Planning grids, adult P.L.O.D. cards, links to 5-14 and the Curriculum for Excellence as it is emerging from the Scottish Government. The CD ROM holds a bank of images and frameworks to create your own P.L.O.D. cards.

Towards a Curriculum for Excellence

In Scotland we are currently in the process of creating and implementing a new curriculum for excellence. In the Curriculum Review one of the principles of curriculum design is progression, which is described as follows:

'Young people should experience continuous progression in their learning from 3 to 18 within a single curriculum framework. Each stage should build upon earlier knowledge and achievements.'

As I write this book there are no final details of the knowledge, skills and attitudes linked to curriculum, but the methodology of teaching and the approach to learning has been clarified and is beginning to inform and change practice in the early stages of education to become much more active. It is our intention to create further curriculum link information for practitioners as they become more defined. Until that point we have included curriculum grids that link to level A 5-14 and the 3-5 curriculum to cover a 3-8 yrs age range.

In response to requests we have published this book about the way to create active learning environments and an accompanying file that supports adults to learn how to support childrens active learning and what type of opportunities to offer to children.

The curriculum for excellence states that children learn by doing, thinking and exploring, and through quality interaction, intervention and relationships, all combining to build the four capacities for each child (detailed on the green diagram). These capacities are at the root of our approach and link very easily to my thinking, which in turn guides the development of Mindstretchers Ltd and all that we do.

The curriculum supports links to parents but also it is important that staff across all early years settings recognise the interests and experiences children bring from home and use these as a starting point to extend learning. Within this book you will see our use of purposeful contexts and how we use formative assessment through the Talking and Thinking Floorbooks to implement active learning that links both adult and child created ideas.

As children progress in their lives, their confidence grows and their skills as independent and co-operative learners develop. They are able to take decisions about their play, at times to initiate it and organise it, and to ask questions and find information. Their experience of a range of learning broadens. They become less reliant on adult support as part of their emotional, personal and social development and become increasingly interested in their friends. They become more able to imagine, concentrate, listen and talk for longer periods. They readily become absorbed in play. They need encouragement from staff to extend their skills, to persevere in solving problems and to widen the scope of activities.

Most children enter primary school as enthusiastic, independent learners who are used to making decisions, solving problems and initiating their own learning. They will bring a range of skills including early literacy and numeracy, and the ability to use these skills in engaging and concentrating during learning activities. They will be eager for new learning to widen their experiences of people, places and nature, and to access and use the written word and mathematical activities, and they will be keen to demonstrate their capabilities in movement, art, music and much more. Many will respond well to stimulating teaching and learning which challenges their thinking.

At the heart of an active learning approach is the creative, adaptable professional who can

'Model making area'

'Mathematical learning out of doors'

develop the ideas that arise when children are immersed in their learning. Staff need to build upon experiences by planning approaches to learning which reflect childrens' enthusiasms, needs and interests. Understanding that play and other forms of active learning are the backbone of learning and teaching in the early years gives shape to the kinds of professional judgements that staff will have to make as children progress through the early level. Direct and interactive teaching will be part of the repertoire of staff from the beginning, although it will become more prominent towards the end of Primary 1. More structured learning should move ahead at a good, enjoyable pace as children's needs dictate.

I hope that teachers and educators become to feel professionally empowered again, so that they are able to move away from an over structured method to one that incorporates childrens thinking, problem solving and activity. This style of approach requires child autonomy and I have suggested ways of achieving this in a busy room with large numbers of children linked to the organisation of time, space, resources and the adult.

Creating the Ethos

Children develop a sense of self image from the feedback they receive from the people around them and the environments they encounter. The environment is made up of a number of things, such as the cleanliness, organisation, décor, and resources. All of which contribute to an atmosphere that gives the message that 'you are important to us and we care about you'. It can also show the method of teaching and learning that you believe in. The active learning approach should be reflected in the entrance way, classrooms and playrooms if they are used.

This section looks at the importance of display and how children should be involved in it. Given that we have already stated that children benefit from a high quality environment because it passes on a subtle message of self worth, let us look at the other benefits of high quality displays.

'Sharing the process of design'

Displays show that you value all the children's efforts.

It is important that the process of learning through play is reflected in the displays. To create a display which illustrates the process of investigating and creating we should highlight the effort that children put into active learning. An example of this would be to put up the print block that the children have made themselves, along with the print experimentation in a variety of shades on a range of materials, accompanied by description or photographs
Centres and schools have developed ways of ensuring that all children have their work on display.

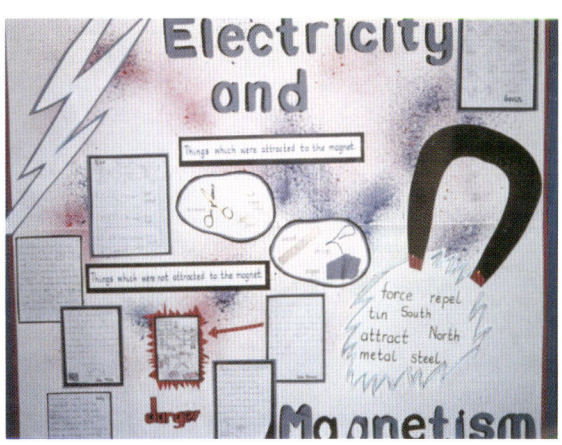
'Sharing frameworks of understanding'

'Investigating literacy'

It is very easy to fall into the trap of displaying the pieces that appeal to the adult eye rather than a child's. Some adults intervene in the creative process to 'gather' pieces of work for a display. A comment that was heard from a child in one group was 'I am not one of the children who get work on the wall' ! Amazing though it may seem, unless there is some form of monitoring and checking, such as individualised picture frames, there may be a similar comment being made in your centre/classroom.

Display encourages observation and curiosity from the children.

Displays should be designed to be touched and handled. To design a display and then ask young children not to touch it or to constantly tidy it up seems to go against the underlying principles of how children learn. If there are delicate items then the display should present them in a protected way so that adult interaction can be geared towards learning as opposed to managing behaviour. There are a number of table designs that have a well in the middle to display fragile items, or a bookcase with perspex doors.

'Sharing creative exploration'

The most effective way of encouraging this observation is to put the display at a height that can be accessed by the children. In situations where display boards are high, small freestanding boards can be brought out so that children can see the pictures and objects at close quarters.

Young children learn through **all** their senses and movement. Display can be much more effective if there are objects and pictures that stimulate a variety of learning mechanisms. Many displays focus on visual 2D objects such as posters and pictures, due to issues of space/resources.

This type of display can be developed with the use of trellis on which to hang things, multisensory 3D objects placed in baskets, and textured backing surfaces. Displays that respond to children's curiosity and interest should evolve and change over a period of time so that the children's developing ideas are reflected through the display. Include a special notice area for 'things we discovered today,' where adults and children can add new observations to the board.

Displays provide information and reminders.

Effective communication between all adults and the children is the key to effective team work. Displays can be part of this communication network. An active classroom has to rely on placing responsibility onto children. Displays that encourage children be more independent e.g. hand washing sequences, work programmes, monitor boards, self registration, consultation boards for ideas are all part of this network.

Stimulating thinking and exploration

Displays should be informative for everyone that reads them so dual language, sign language, photographs displaying different learning styles should all be included. Displays can work on a variety of different levels. Captions of the thinking behind the task can work for visitors and parents to the school, whereas the photographs and work will give positive feedback to the children. To be effective as a communication board the displays should give out clear messages about the school. The message can be obvious or more subtle. There are some positive and negative examples given below.

Adult drawn displays

Displays are often presented in a way which appears to claim that the work is all the children's own creative response. If the work on the display has been drawn by adults and coloured with pre-made single colour paint what will the message be? It could be suggested that the group feels that children's work isn't good enough for the displays, so the adults make decisions for the children and essentially structure the work so highly that the children have little or no ownership of the work. This autocratic way of working should have no place in the collaborative environment of an early years environment. If adults wish to put up their own work they should accept that they are doing just that, rather than pretending to show children's work.

What is displayed and how it is displayed has a strong influence on the formation of the children's attitudes and values.

Too much clutter and mess around the display gives an underlying message that the area is not really important. Notices that are spelt wrongly or that are poorly written do the same. The quality of a display should be the same when it is taken down as when it went up.

'Displays should be clear and uncluttered'

Children are very good at picking up underlying messages from adults. They may never say anything since the shift can be attitudinal and therefore longer term. In many environments the display areas are planned such that all aspects of the curriculum are represented, (not just 'art'), all children have work on display at all times, the displays change on a regular basis, all members of staff take turns to put a display up, regular maintenance of the display retains quality, and training is given in the techniques of creating a display.

'Valuing anecdotal and personal connections to learning'

Children should have an involvement in the creation of the displays.

Asking children what they think would make a great display often results in very interesting feedback. Children as young as 3 or 4 can be taught to use a safety trimmer (the style with guidelines to assist alignment). The process of putting up the display can be a learning opportunity for discussing colour, pattern, size, fixings, etc. Choice of the backing/mounting paper shades and the creation of a drape can all be made by the children.

The type of display where work is put onto the wall immediately, rather than 2-3 days later, is of great value to children. There are a variety of materials on the market, such as no-stick paper mounts designed to hold light weight cards and which do not require pins, magnetic boards, bulldog clips, and cup hooks, which will all give children complete autonomy to create their own displays and communication centres. Some centres place these displays by the creative area, in the role play area and near specific areas such as writing areas.

Children can create drapes that reflect their interests and style of art. There are a huge variety of fabric markers and paints on the market that will allow centres to wash the fabrics. Methods for storing drapes are well worth developing so that displays are not held back for want of the ironing process e.g. coat hangers on a dress rail.

Create different levels so that the eye sees a range of objects across the display. The boxes that store your artifacts can be used, so that when it comes to taking the display down all the boxes are at hand.

Displays are an important part of the early years environment, but there should be a balance between too much window dressing and more collaboration with the children in the centre. Some displays take weeks to create, by which time the moment has passed and the children cannot remember what the display is all about. Immediate displays are exciting to create, since the look on the child's face is often enough to tell you how proud and special they feel at that moment.

'Child created display'

'Mark making materials on offer in work boxes'

'Creative area set up for self help'

Harmonisation to Create a Curriculum for Excellence

'To be a real learner, you have to want to learn. People who want to learn generally enjoy it, are actively engaged in it, and will experiment freely with materials or contexts, and choose how and what to approach to enhance their learning. This is a playful approach to learning, and the vital approach for all children to become successful and active participants in the learning process.'

Moyles 1991

Developing a curriculum which offers learning and teaching through play based/experiential opportunities means that the adults who plan what the curriculum is, and how it should be delivered, need to have an understanding of what play can offer.

The word curriculum has a broad range of definitions that are of significance to a range of people. In the broadest view it is a planned programme of opportunities that meet the needs of children. So we can suggest that life is a curriculum, that everything in a babies' life is learning. In order to create balance and coherence, most countries have developed curricula to focus adults in their teaching and learning. The curriculum of a place gives a window into the priorities and beliefs of that society. Some are more based around natural life skills such as Montessori, others focus on cultural interdependence such as Te Whakiriki in New Zealand, some on emotional wellbeing as seen in Sweden.

'Moving the curriculum into a variety of spaces'

There have been a few curriculum documents that have had an influence on the methodology in Scotland. These are currently being harmonised to become a Curriculum for Excellence 3-18. People view that the recorded document that explores the 3-5 year old experiences is totally play based, and another termed the 5-14 curriculum is viewed as more structured. Yet when both documents are read in detail they support a balance of teaching and learning methods which leads to an experiential method of learning, where children are encouraged to reflect on their own learning within a structured space, with clear teaching objectives to ensure progression and challenge. This section examines the way in which we could harmonise the experiences of children so that the learning pathways are consistent and therefore more effective.

The 3-5 curriculum looks at the balance of skills and knowledge within a framework that is subdivided into 5 areas:

- Emotional Personal and Social Development with an emphasis on self belief and inner confidence.
- Communication and Language which includes all types of communication.
- Knowledge and Understanding of the World has been used as an umbrella term over Science, Mathematics and Technology. It does reflect the focus in the early years to put mathematics into context rather than discrete skills.
- Expressive and Aesthetic Development, which acknowledges all forms of expression in young children.
- Physical Development and Movement that emphasise the need for activity and movement in the learning process.

The curriculum is relevant to all the childcare environments that are available such as childminders, nursery, educare centres, playgroups and schools.

The overall aim is that children have a range and breadth of 3-5 experiences that are active, challenging and broad based.

These divisions move on to the 5-14 curriculum:

- Emotional Personal and Social Development extends into Religious and Moral Education and Health.
- Communication and Language extends into English Language which covers key aspects of the different Genre.
- Knowledge and Understanding of the World presents the document through approaches to finding out about Social Science and Technology.
- Mathematics becomes a discrete subject with clear aspects of mathematical knowledge highlighted.
- Physical Development and Movement in it's widest form becomes Expressive Arts which looks at Physical Education, Music and Drama, Dance, Visual and Aesthetic Art.

The 5-14 documents all state that the subdivisions should overlap, with subjects such as drama being used as a learning medium to deliver other areas of the curriculum. There are clear guidelines set out in the methodology section that state that these areas of learning should be presented in a variety of methods such as discussion, exposition, enquiry, and problem solving (ref. e.g. Mathematics 5-14). The methods used to present the curriculum cover the 5 key principles such as Breadth, Balance, Continuity, Coherence, and Progression and it is in these apparently simple words that we find a huge variation in their interpretation. A school in Perth and Kinross has an outdoor classroom that is timetabled for use throughout the year. The continuity is such that all children have outdoor experiences from the nursery through to P7. The methods they have developed in the school support a balanced style of direct teaching with experiential learning through play both inside and out.

The third type of curriculum is referred to as the null curriculum. It covers the hidden aspects of the curriculum that convey the values and beliefs of the setting. It is the most powerful aspect of the learning environment in that it sets up feelings of self worth, value, commitment and perseverance. All these attitudes and beliefs interweave with the knowledge aspects of learning and have a long lasting effect on the learner.

The null curriculum is conveyed through staff attitude, adult interaction, group expectations, social language, peer interaction and behaviour, organisation of space, time and resources, and the very methods the teachers use to teach.

The approach to children learning in the early stages is based on key principles.

The curriculum is a blend of skills, knowledge, and attitudes that carry on through life long learning.

'Working in a variety of social groups'

Any aspect of these are of equal importance and should have a place in our schools. Some regions and indeed, countries, have placed percentage blocks of time onto the curriculum to monitor breadth and balance. The learning process is actually holistic since the brain draws on all aspects of its capability to solve problems or apply knowledge in a creative way. The curriculum offers adults a clear route to presenting a block of information or skills that we want to introduce to children but it cannot guarantee assimilation or accommodation of the new information for each child if the method of teaching is inappropriate to the child. This process happens when children develop a deeper understanding that can only occur through application and often physical involvement such as play. Forman and Cadzean (1985).

The process of learning is as important as a product that has come from it.

Measuring play has always offered a challenge due to the transient nature of it. The methods suggested in this book involve children in the process of recording their thinking and process of learning through photographs etc, so that the nature of experiential learning is kept intact.

'Sand as a sensorial space for mathematics'

Children are individuals and are part of a larger community.

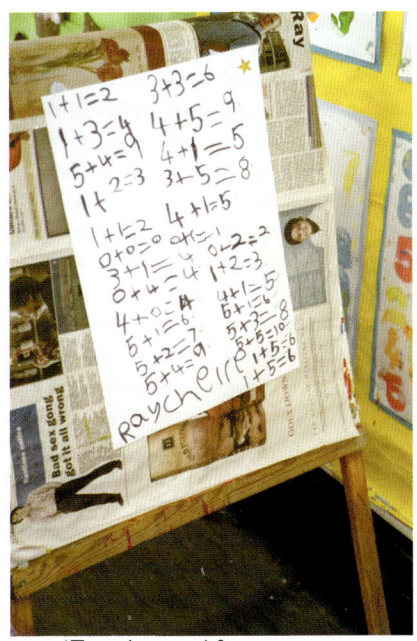
'Easels used for numeracy as well as art'

Children are individuals and bring a range of experiences and competencies to both childcare and the early education stages. It is important that the practitioners create an environment within which children can learn in a variety of ways according to their need.

The curriculum should be presented in meaningful ways.

The contexts that are presented to children should be meaningful and relevant so that children can place the information within existing frameworks of understanding. In our centres these are presented through effective, responsive planning delivered through experiential learning. In our schools these should continue to be integrated into work programmes to enable children to apply their learning. The curriculum for excellence has four elements beneath it which are detailed overleaf. These fit very closely to the approaches we have mentioned above.

A Curriculum for Excellence

Successful Learners

with

- enthusiasm and motivation for learning
- determination to reach high standards of achievement
- openness to new thinking and ideas

and able to

- use literacy, communication and numeracy skills
- use technology for learning
- think creatively and independently
- learn independently and as part of a group
- make reasoned evaluations
- link and apply different types of learning in new situations

Confident Individuals

with

- self-respect
- a sense of physical, mental and emotional wellbeing
- secure values and beliefs
- ambition

and able to

- relate to others and manage themselves
- pursue a healthy and active lifestyle
- be self-aware
- develop and communicate their own beliefs and view of the world
- live as independently as they can assess risk and take informed decisions
- achieve success in different areas of activity

To enable all young people to become:

Responsible Citizens

with

- respect for others
- commitment to participate responsibly in political, economic, social and cultural life

and able to

- develop knowledge and understanding of the world and Scotland's place in it
- understand different beliefs and cultures
- make informed choices and decisions
- evaluate environmental, scientific and technological issues
- develop informed, ethical views of complex issues

Effective Contributors

with

- an enterprising attitude
- resilience
- self-reliance

and able to

- communicate in different ways and in different settings
- work in partnership and in teams
- take the initiative and lead
- apply critical thinking in new contexts
- create and develop
- solve problems

18 Learning Pathways

Curriculum and Experiential Learning
Exploring Teaching and Learning Through Play

The term 'play' has suffered from the fact that it can be applied to a wide variety of experiences. Theorists have tried to clarify it, define terms and tried to quantify it through statistics. There are still a huge variety in the play provision across our centres from the naturalistic Montessori schools through to seat based didactic experiences favoured by the Victorians!

In order to manage large groups of children we have changed and altered space, time and resources to structure these experiences.

'Rich role play experiences'

Pelligrini suggested the idea of a continuum of structure that enables the practitioner to consider how much structure they provide in different experiences. It appeared that construction had little structure and creativity had the most! Some of these approaches encourage extended learning and others have created segregated and minimised learning to be no more than a 'tag on' after 'real learning' has taken place.

Play can be organised in a variety of different ways such as through:

- Areas of play such as sand, water, construction, role play.
- Through skill based opportunities such as those presented in Partners in Learning (Strathclyde) or Montessori.
- Single knowledge based areas, linked to the curriculum documents i.e. the maths area.
- Open areas which cross over organisational boundaries to be totally child centred where resources are used wherever they are required.
- Play according to physical layout of rooms such as messy play, clean play, physical play.
- Random resources held in a separate playroom.
- Outcome/knowledge based planning presented in a playful way.

The list could go on.

The underlying issues need to be identified if we are to justify the place of active learning in a curricula orientated environment. To say that they are involved with messy play, does not identify learning or the real benefits of the experience to the child.

The evidence we now have about the brain should be taken on board and then influence what we do with children. The bibliography at the end of the file is full of references to people who are analysing what we do and how children retain the information. Daniel Goleman looks at the effect of emotional intelligence on our life long learning and the element which features highly within that, is personal self belief and motivation, both of which are high within play orientated experiences.

The following pages attempt to unpick the different emphasis that is placed on the child and the way they learn in a child centred space, and in an environment that can be curriculum led but is delivered in an active way.

Child Centred

Suggested opportunities and strategies for child centred play based curriculum in the early years

- Promote ownership through involvement in planning by sharing ideas and thinking. This can be through simple discussions, picture lists, verbal outpouring (Reggio approach), Mind Maps© (Buzan), 3D maps, or recorded talk in a Talking and Thinking book©. (Warden) or the Drama approach (Bilbao).

- Develop ownership of the physical layout of the play areas from the creation of the resources to the building of the enclosure . This can be through designing and making items to go into the role play area, slowing down the process to give more depth and quality to the things they create. The implicit message is that the thinking, the process of creating is the most important thing.

- Create an Environment of Choice. Play involves decision making and trying to make informed choices given a variety of 2D and 3D resources, or choice about how to approach a challenge. Two colours of paint, that must not be mixed, does not give a great deal of choice.

- Promote individuality, with each child creating/making their own learning. Individual talking and thinking books enables children to look back at their thinking and see what they have learnt and found out themselves through play/experiential learning. Personal development plans create individual targets/next steps for improvement in all aspects.

- Promote partnership and collaboration between children, and adults so that children do not constantly receive information and answers but explore and experiment to find out their own frameworks of understanding about all aspects of the curriculum.

- Find motivation. Everyone has a motivational button that will start to inspire, enthuse and encourage them to persevere with challenges. The freedom of play to experiment and explore free from a 'correct 'answer is a powerful tool.

- Ensure there are connected play experiences, so that children see the larger picture and can then apply and test their ideas over a longer block of time.

- Play needs time so that ideas can develop and deepen. Create flexibility for interests to develop over a period of days.

- Offer a variety of sensorial zones to enable children to engage fully in the learning process.

Curriculum

Suggested opportunities and strategies for a curriculum based environment which is delivered in an active way

- Create experiential learning tasks linked to direct teaching from 3 - 18 years. Cluster schools are working together to create joint resources for children 3-7 years.

- Develop the approach over time so that adults can share their ideas as the children respond, thus building up a larger more relevant bank of opportunities. Schools and centres have created development plans that are based on a five year pathway. This allows assimilation of an active approach into the ethos of the school.

- Differentiate the tasks through expectation of learning, resources, time for completion, to ensure progression and therefore continuous learning.

- Store the above in a central store so that all staff in the primary school can easily access the equipment or ideas.

- Look at the organisation and management in the rooms to make space for well organised, relevant resources so that children can develop their independence. Encourage children to spread out and move around freely so that there are periods of movement and seat-based work.

- Examine the theme work or programmes of study and develop resource packs to support these aspects of the curriculum during structured activity time. The creation of Talking Tubs™ enables staff to focus the learning whilst also consulting children about their existing knowledge. The ideas that children provide can then become part of the active learning programme.

- Examine tasks or activities that are child initiated, and cross reference them to the curriculum so that children are at the centre of the decision making process. Staff need to plan when to interact to support and extend learning.

- Create methods of feedback that respond to visual, auditory and kinaesthetic learners rather than always written/colouring-in worksheets (refer to the assessment section).

- Consider assessment in its widest form and include more self assessment through the play process.

- Consider the awareness of the adults working with the children. Their interaction and the value they place on the experience should be of a high quality and be consistent.

The Curriculum for Excellence brings together the delivery of the curriculum in a play-based or active way.

As suggested in *'Building the Curriculum 3-18 (2): Active Learning in the Early Years'*; "Active learning is learning which engages and challenges children's thinking using real-life and imaginary situations. It takes full advantage of the opportunities for learning presented by:

- spontaneous play
- planned, purposeful play
- investigating and exploring
- building on events and life experiences
- focused learning and teaching"

Within this document, a series of principles are identified which enable effective active learning. These are:

- progression in children's development and learning
- supporting continuity in learning and development
- the environment for learning, staff and resources
- the involvement of parents
- continuing professional development.

Progression and supported continuity of learning and development are closely linked. Active learning must ensure the succession of learning. In order to do this adults need to be able to identify the next steps for the learning pathway to move on or broaden. These next steps may use the same resources, but be differentiated by the expectation of the adult or indeed differentiated through outcome. This encourages children to set their own extended goals through critical thinking skills/floor book session or asking open ended questions which support children in developing new ideas or theories to test. Children must be motivated to develop these ideas otherwise interest can be lost in the opportunity.

A key factor with ACE (A Curriculum for Excellence) is the requirement to support continuity in learning and development in moving from Nursery to Primary 1. Using similar zones of learning to the nursery for active play increases the emotional security and therefore the confidence of children. Working co-operatively with colleagues to develop similar language and approaches to learning during active play can also ease these transitions.

To creating an environment for active learning *'Building the Curriculum 3-18 (2): Active Learning in the Early Years'*; suggests four vital components: the use of space; active learning outdoors; resources and time. These are addressed in detail in this book.

Finally it is vital to involve parents and support staff in their professional development regarding active learning. Parents are often supportive of increased activity when their children display increased motivation and a desire to talk over their learning in the home environment. This can only be because the learning experiences have struck a chord within them.

Staff are already using elements of active learning during mathematics, language and environmental studies lessons. The next step is to link this up with a more consistent approach, slowly building up the active learning provision they provide at a pace that suits them and their children. Through linking the activity zones to core teaching the whole environment becomes more engaging for a greater proportion of the time.

Organisation and Management

Young children need to feel that they are in an environment that is organised and managed to meet their needs and those of the adult. Large desks for teachers to sit at, have a limited use for children apart from knowing where to queue!! Resources that are permanently stacked away are being controlled, and short bursts of play experiences can lead to superficial learning.

This section supports practitioners in creating an experiential area for young children to learn. There should be a continuity and flow between types of early years provision, unfortunately there are many children who try to follow the likes and dislikes of individual teachers and the places they work. Some of these children 'unlearn independence skills' to fit into the new group way of working.

'Shared open area for active learning'

Let us consider the challenges that some children have to face during a transition between an experiential environment to a didactic, adult lead space. The transition may happen between home and centre, or centre and school and be in either direction. The key is to have harmonisation between all the learning environments in the early years, with a collective understanding of the way that children learn.

'Well structured role play writing area'

- Choice to find which resources you feel you want *vs Resources presented and chosen by the adult.*

- Time to explore the materials and to create something that you are happy with *vs Production of a number of half hearted attempts with little quality.*

- Ownership of learning with greater personal motivation *vs receiving information with possibly a low retention rate due to low emotional connection.*

- Resources that challenge and inspire *vs adult designed equipment that switches off enthusiasm.*

- Active, critical thinkers that challenge everybody's thinking including adults *vs Compliant children who develop learned helplessness and receive information through worksheets, without critical thought.*

The organisation of the learning environment is something that is critical to the effectiveness of learning itself. Time, space, people and the resources themselves are all integral to the process.

Time

Time is the one thing that many practitioners feel steals away quality interactions and depth of learning. In order to make more effective use of time we need to examine how it is being spent at the moment, because something *is* happening. In a recent survey regarding use of time in one classroom the teacher was shocked to hear the amount of time children stood waiting in queues to see her. In order to release time we sometimes need to make changes to our practice or methodology of teaching and learning.

'Child with access to sand & water'

An effective learning environment should ensure that:

- Children understand the structure of the day.

- Children are given choice in how to use time within that structure.

- Children are given the opportunity to progress at a rate appropriate to their readiness.

- Daily patterns are flexible to allow for spontaneous development.

- The learning process has time for repetition and consolidation built in.

- Staff manage time effectively, so that they interact with children.

- Outdoor areas are accessible and used throughout the year for learning.

- Children have access to quality time.

The lack of time is often the greatest barrier to staff who feel that targets have to be met and the percentage time allotted to key subjects prevents experiential learning. Some schools have managed to find a pathway through the barriers to create a positive place to learn that is based on sound learning and teaching strategies. These practical ideas are noted on the support pages.

'Purposeful activity with adult support'

Suggested Opportunities and Strategies to Use Time Effectively

Time is finite, so the only way to create more quality time means reducing the amount of time used for other activities that are secondary to the planned learning opportunities such as interruptions, administration of information and allocation of resources.

Interruptions

- Interruptions break up time, and can be avoided by setting up clear systems for the management of children and adults.

- Create do not disturb signs for the door.

- Put up a notice board for school staff to leave messages on, so you can pick them up later.

- Create a working agreement not to pop in to tell people messages unless urgent.

- In small schools with little secretarial support, answer machines are used effectively in sessions and checked at breaks.

- Wear a hat, badge that shows children they are not to disturb you at group teaching time/focus time.

- Have a secret sign, such as tap their arm for leaving the room to go to the toilet (or **don't have a sign at all**).

- Set up simple morning routines supported by easy access and use resources.

Sharing Information

- Create clear picture cues in sequence so that children know what tasks to go on to.

- Create individual/group activity lines with pictures of tasks/symbols as memory joggers.

- Train children to go to each other for support.

'Creating a record of choices'

- Put a display easel on the table to **remind children what they should be doing** i.e. working on their own, working in pairs, with the teacher.

- Registration/lunches etc can take up time. Staff can create a series of methods that can be used throughout the early years such as putting an object or picture from one place to another; self registration with blocks, posting name card through a postbox.

Allocation/Collecting of Resources

- Create group completion trays, boxes or work in progress although worktops and surfaces can be more effectively used for an active task. Books can be put away in drawer units rather than in class piles.

- Have carry handle boxes on each table that hold core resources that can be easily cleared off for experiential learning/play.

- Use monitors to give out resources.

- Create well labelled areas with relevant materials in the classroom, store other items in the main store cupboard.

'Sequence charts'

- Create linked resource boxes so that the classroom can be quickly changed and modified to respond to different curricula areas e.g. Role play bags (see resource ideas).

- Schools and centres can work together to share common resources as the amount of active learning in the early stages increases. This approach needs to be monitored to ensure that the quality of the resources is maintained within the shared box.

- In schools where they have adopted the Talking Tubs™ as an approach to formative assessment and engagement of children in pre-determined contexts, it can be effective to create network or cluster groups to share ideas and sources of material.

'Self registration'

'Interactive displays set up near activity zone to stimulate talking & thinking'

Relevance of Existing Use of Time

Some opportunities that are used for teaching and learning take up a lot of time that could be used for activity. Staff need to look at the quality of experience within the time-frame. Low order thinking should be minimised to make way for higher order active involvement e.g. reduce the amount of colouring in, minimise the use of cutting and sticking to demonstrate knowledge.

Resources

Resources - Materials and Equipment

The organisation of materials and equipment is fundamental to the smooth running of an early years environment. Children and adults need to know where objects are stored if they are going to be able to be responsive to young children. Many classroom spaces have limited scope for resource presentation so the photographs are from a range of environments that do not have the ideal space.

In an effective learning environment resources should:

- Be accessible to everyone. Resources can be shared across the early years environment 3-8 so widening the range of resources.

- Encourage self help skills and independence throughout the early years. Learning should not be rigidly compartmentalised, many resources encourage skills that transfer from one curricular area to another. Selection and choice develop autonomy, and with that comes confidence.

- Offer choice and a range of materials to suit the variety of learning styles - a variety of visual, auditory and kinaesthetic.

- Represent a multi-cultural society through all the resources, not only at festivals/events.

- Be multisensory to respond to different types of learner - explore the possibilities of 'real' materials rather than plastic.

'Home made resources'

- Be carefully chosen to enhance and support the curriculum. Resources are selected for their learning potential in relation to the curriculum for excellence.

- Be labelled according to stage of development with a mixture of object, picture, silhouette and word. Progression should be built into all aspects of the learning process, including labelling of resources.

- Be attractive, of good quality, and relevant.

- Be adaptable, open ended and flexible.

- Challenge children's thinking to support progression.

Suggested Opportunities And Strategies To Use Resources Effectively

- Clearly labelled containers at child height.

- Labels that vary their form - picture/word/symbol as child develops.

- Easy to open storage such as plastic sweet jars, cookie pots.

- Wall space used for storage such as DIY boards with containers clipped on, pillowcases hanging on a pole for junk store.

'Well organised self check systems for resources'

- Shoe tidy with clear pockets hanging on shelving during activity sessions.

- Wardrobe shoe store lying on its back for wools, paper etc - put a tag of colour on each section to aid clearing away.

- Picture/silhouette on the shelf to aid tidying away.

- Variety of resources on offer all the time to be used in cross curricular ways. e.g. balls of clay in a pot with hessian mats to work on, re-cycled paper bin, small solid paints for detailed work.

- A variety of resources that enable children to represent their thinking in a variety of ways such as crayon, pencil, charcoal, paint, rulers, textured papers etc.

- Areas for sensorial play such as sand, water, leaves, grass turf etc all presented through a drawer unit, rather than always in a sand pit.

- Malleable resources such as the clay, play dough, plastic modelling materials with a range of tools to support the activity in a modelling box (feathers, bark, rollers, tweezers, buttons, pipe cleaners).

- Fix it box containing a variety of glues, sellotape, masking tape, paper clips, large elastic bands, string. So that it can be taken to any area and used in learning.

- Discovery den containing investigative tools for the exploration inside and out. Cardboard box fit for two, or a divider large enough for 1 will automatically limit numbers.

- Transient equipment that can be brought out into classrooms to create a more play based environment, e.g.. Role play bags with fabric, paper, equipment linked to a theme so that it can be set up by the children on or under the tables.

'Commercial and child created resources'

- Create writing opportunities in a briefcase that contains all the resources required for an office area, an autumn den with leaf books and carved pens, a winter ice world with cold coloured paper and snowflakes to write on.

- Limit the number of waistcoats, hats, or bands to manage numbers in one or two areas, at the beginning, then try to encourage children's social skills by understanding how it feels to be in a crush in the home corner, so that they self limit and organise.

- Make natural connections between resources such as play dough in the home corner, fabrics in the construction area and water outside.

- Take photographs of children creating/using resources to support other children to develop ideas. If children have not met a resource before it is an effective way of sharing the potential of the material.

- Look at all the resources available generally from 3-8 years. Consider the progression and challenge in the actual resource itself. Materials trays vary enormously. 3-5 years could be larger perhaps and floor based. The 5-6 years could be transparent/opaque with slopes. 6-7 years could be transparent with a variety of locks, mechanisms and levels. 7-8 years could be transparent with water filters, pumps, syphons, mechanisms, clips and measures.

- Take photographs of children creating/using resources to support other children to develop ideas. If children have not met a resource before it is an effective way of sharing the potential of the material.

- Children should be challenged to deepen learning. The correct use of core resources can of course be influenced by adult direction/consultation to agree joint goals.

- Use open-ended materials such as the den fabrics to create enclosures - differentiate by alternating the fabrics in the bag e.g. chiffon is hard to handle in comparison to a blanket.

'Den areas created with buckets & poles'

Space

In effective learning environments the space element creates welcoming, inviting and stimulating learning bays to attract children and adults into the early years environment.

"The integrated nature of children's learning means that the class space has to be flexible and dynamic, with each designated area capable of a wide variety of different types of activity"

Moyles 1991

'Space to create group play/activity'

An integrated approach to learning requires organisation of space so that it can be maximised. The nature of some Primary 1 classes is such that they do not have a table and chair for each child, because there are always groups of children busy investigating on the move.

It is very easy to settle into a space and use it in the same way every year. Team up with other practitioners to look at the large resources you have and how you can use them to best effect.

In order to create effective teaching and learning it is vital to provide:

'Access to indoor & outdoor space for learning'

- Areas of enclosure so that children feel able to engage with adults.

- Space to explore materials, both indoors and out.

- Quiet secluded areas which offer the security to develop perseverance and concentration. Many children (as many as 1 in 4) suffer from hearing loss at some point. We need to consider the noise that large, open spaces create.

- Space to display their own work. A positive ethos is important to convey the 'null' curriculum. High standards of display from staff will give a message of self worth and value to the children, encourage curiosity, consolidate learning, and communicate values and beliefs to parents.

- Opportunities to work with friends, or groups so that they can create their own social boundaries.

- Larger areas of space for bigger equipment or larger groupings of children.

- Areas at different height levels to enable the children to view the activities/resources from different perspectives.

Suggested Opportunities And Strategies To Use Space Effectively

'Cozy spaces to encourage reading'

- Tidy up, organise and discard old or irrelevant resources!

- Prioritise the resources that are taking up space so that they can be used for a number of different areas of the curriculum.

- Find flexible ways of subdividing space, such as screens, so that they can be used to respond to the needs of children.

- Use low bookcases, storage units, low photograph boards, plants to subdivide space.

- Use bed canopies, drapes, interfacing, ribbons to create hanging dividers (may be unhooked from ceiling at night to avoid alarms).

- Fix trellis to the back of units/hang from wall or ceiling to give a more rigid divider.

- Division of space on a table top with masking tape/coloured tape to divide opportunities for a personal space for working.

- Create a range of opportunities for the presentation of resources, so that there is a variety of space. E.g. natural materials such as sand, individual trays for use on table tops, gravel trays for paired work, small sand tray for group work and outside sand area to walk into for large group.

- Create visual barriers to outline space such as individual learning mats, group play mats and whole class listening mats to avoid children walking through the floor play.

- Label drawers with word and picture, see through containers, open topped containers, individual bag systems to use outside that all enable choice and selection.

- Allow access to well structured outside area with zones for areas of the curriculum. Support this with a simple transportation system that provides the small equipment to deepen quality of play and learning.

'Provision of table top & floor based activity'

- Make effective use of 'dead spaces' such as corridors, old cloakrooms, tops of units, teachers tables. Consider the removal of doors from old cupboards to reduce the need for dead space in front of the doors.

Learning Pathways

- Install trapezium/angled bookcases in long corridors to slow down children and create display areas.

- Create systems for the routines, to allow you to remove the teachers desk. The space it takes up is not only the table itself but the space around it for the queues of children. A chair may be enough with teacher resources in a store box. Books can be collected into tote boxes, finished work into a tray for marking.

- Exploration of materials usually creates mess and perhaps noise, alleviate concern about this by having clear tidy up routines with small sized tools at hand, a piece of carpet on the wood work bench to reduce noise.

'An old cupboard transformed'

- Create space for display by using banners that can be hung up during play sessions e.g. a backdrop of a wood land, a snowy place etc. These can then be rolled up and put away.

- Create childrens' display areas with hooks, 'Grip strip'®, or self stick fabric used for Christmas cards.

- Some environments have created learning walls to provide a focus for children's exploration and investigation. The information on the wall can then be transferred to a book format for long term use.

- Reduce the quantity of each resource and extend the variety.

- Use 'toy hammocks' to increase storage for light weight materials.

- Catalogue resources into hanging bags (clear) and locate on a moveable hanging rail.

- Use pulley systems to store resources up high – so that they can be lowered when required.

'Use of storage top to provide interactive learning spaces that stimulate talking & thinking'

- Utilize sides of cupboards, filing cabinets for display surfaces/organisation points.

People

Practitioners are the greatest resource. This aspect of the document will focus on the management of a variety of play areas and the use of adults to staff them. Roles and responsibilities should be referred to in individual regional documents.

The first question we need to address is whether an adult needs to be with a child for learning to take place. Anyone who has seen a child watch a butterfly emerging knows how potent it is as a learning strategy. The learning can be enhanced, focused, guided, extended, but unless there is a match between the level of expectation and the opportunity given, some adult interactions can limit or even misdirect a child's learning.

Knowledgeable adults who are aware of the value of play can deepen learning through the provision of resources, changing length of time for activity, giving space and most importantly through their interaction and affirmation of the whole experience.

'Interacting to guide and focus'

'Interaction to widen awareness of knowledge/skill'

The one aspect that is constant about the role of the adult in play environments is that it has to be as a manager or a scaffolder. There are a great many theories of play that have different implications for classroom/centre practice. However Moyles (1994) clarifies the evidence that play based curricula can *raise standards* when three main strands are effective: the quality of provision, the value associated with active processes, and the involvement of adults.

The Department of Education and Science place great emphasis on the presence of 'sensitive, knowledgeable and informed adult involvement and intervention' to gain the true value of play experiences in schools. This involvement is based on careful observation of children's activities to facilitate assessment and planning for continuity and progression.

Consistency across the adult behaviours in the learning environment lead to a greater sense of trust and security in the early years. Fair, supportive, interested adults create a positive ethos for learning.

Suggested Opportunities And Strategies For The Effective Use Of Adults

- Clarify roles, responsibilities, balance of work so that no one person feels over-laden and resentful. Many people creating resources will make the task much easier.

- Set clear expectations that all the classes using a shared space adhere to; helping tidy up, use of materials, re-stocking, levels of behaviour when active so that the quality of area is maintained.

- Create clear timetables for use of a joint area as a team, to ensure that it fits into each classroom week.

- Involve parents, classroom assistants, teachers, nursery nurses, carers, the janitor, in other words the whole team, so that their strengths are used to benefit the area.

- Create joint ownership between school, adults and children so that they take care of the area.

'Interaction to support children emotionally'

- Involve children in the choice and purchase of equipment, layout etc through talking and thinking books.

- Provide support for adults working in the area, through training so that they have a working understanding of a play area and its value in the learning process.

- Provide support cards that identify learning/purpose of task/outcome to support less confident adults and to focus interaction on learning.

- Create multi-cultural resources in dual language, use familiar resources in the play context to respond to diversity.

- Create the opportunity for adults to be involved in a variety of ways. During the play session, after or in the preparation of it.

- The lead adult should have the overview of the development of the opportunities to ensure progression.

- Use team planning to create opportunities that will cross over aspects of the curriculum (see case study 2) to share responsibility.

- Create resource bags that have contents, task cards and guides to make the process of set up and checking easier and more efficient.

Planning For Play

The planning process should contribute towards the effectiveness of the learning experience through creating a closer match between the needs of the children and the provision. The basis of the planning should be observation and interaction with children, to identify a clear focus and purpose for the opportunity. Through the use of a curriculum framework made up of skills, attitudes, knowledge and concepts the breadth and balance of learning experiences can be monitored. Short term planning should involve a range of teaching and learning methodology, that respond to individual learning styles, previous learning, stage of development, and motivation.

Fabian (2002) identifies five ways that teachers can plan for play
- Plan to promote specific skills
- Plan outcomes from specific areas such as role play
- Plan for progression and challenge
- Plan interactions by informing them of the learning intentions.
- Plan structured play into the day (rather than one slot a week)

In early years units the planning should be more responsive than in school situations where time-tabling, stage of understanding, and pressure of time and space will lead to more structure in the play opportunities.

The Learning Pathways framework file is for teachers to use within the two Scottish documents that are the 3-5 and the 5-14 curriculum. The organisation is under the areas of the new Curriculum for Excellence with the underlying skills, concepts, knowledge identified so that it can be used by practitioners in all early years environments. A detailed example of the grids are provided in this section related to mathematics.

Plan For Skills.

Some active environments focus on the development of skills such as communication, organisation and investigation, since these skills cut across the knowledge content of a set curriculum (Warden 1999).

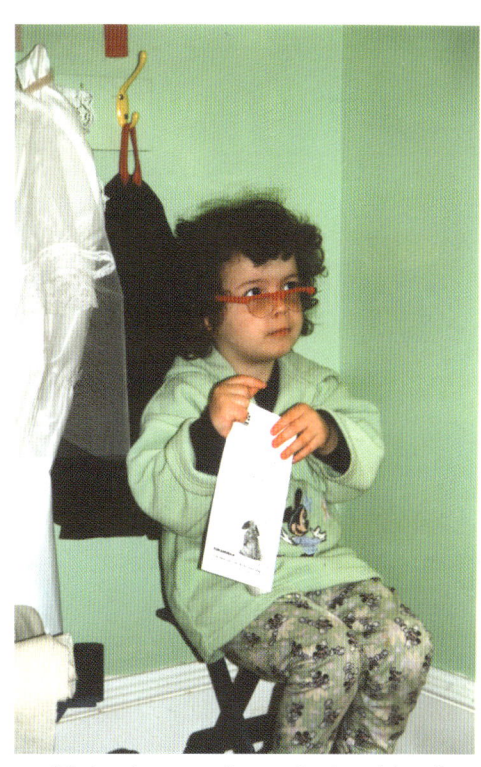

'Role play as a focus for teaching & learning'

Plan For Outcomes From Specific Areas Such As Role Play.

Role Play is a method of learning and can therefore be utilised to teach any outcome whether knowledge, skills or attitudes. The staff can focus on an outcome through the provision of resources and if required a prop to prompt activity e.g. a box arrives with 'ancient relics' or a letter requests help from the children to catalogue the artefacts and create a storage system. The outcome would be to raise awareness of the role of the archaeologist, classification systems and problem solving to create the box.

Plan For Progression And Challenge In Play...Differentiation Through Outcome.

Progression in play and learning is important if children are to develop and deepen their understanding of concepts. In terms of planning experiences the implication of this is to slow down the number of experiences in the structured area, through small changes in the provision. These changes can be pre-thought out, prepared for and then used flexibly in response to observation and assessment.

An example could be based in the water tray and be resource lead. (Possible mathematical learning).

Water clear, precious stones of similar size, laid out near by.
(number of stones in a hand)
Introduction of containers of various sizes.
(larger numbers, volume)
Change of water to cloudy.
(estimation of how many will you catch in your hand, out of water count to check)
Introduction of tiny fishing nets.
(increase number size and therefore talk)
Larger pieces of fabric and garden wire to make own net.
(increase number size again. Measures and problem solving in the net making)
Larger stones and shells.
(value to objects discussion ..larger greater value.)
Introduce value cards 1 shell worth 5, 1 rock worth 10.
(cumulative addition)

'Big plans to stimulate spatial logical diagrams'

Plan Interactions By Informing Them Of The Learning Intention.

The same resources are used over a series of experiences, the differentiation can be introduced through verbal expectation and interaction, or pictorial/word P.L.O.D. cards. Learning is recorded in the Talking and Thinking book (A chinagraph pencil and a laminated sheet for the water tray is often easier at the beginning).

The P.L.O.D. cards have clear learning intentions so that children are aware of the purpose and focus of *some* play opportunities. Even though the intention is given, it still allows differentiation by outcome.

Support for some children who find independent learning challenging can be provided through considered planning such as classroom assistants, older children, focus teaching by the teacher in the experiential/play area, parental support. In classrooms where the play can be integrated, well structured experiences are self fulfilling and the movement of the teacher from a defined teaching area at intervals through the work programme is often enough.

'Small scale resources can spread to create wonderful spaces'

Planning Structured Play Into The Day

Creating time for structured play or experiential learning in classrooms, and joint play areas requires some planning so that maximum use is made of the space and availability.

The amount we know about the way children learn has taken a leap forward, methodology is now being influenced by Howard Gardners theory of multiple intelligences; Daniel Goleman's work on Emotional Intelligence; Alasdair Smith's work on accelerated learning; Tony Buzan and mind mapping; all of which have a root in scientific understanding of the brain. More importantly where practitioners have been lead down a route of seat based, didactic teaching in small discrete blocks, they are now being given the chance to assert their deep rooted belief in the need for supported learning; creating connections; providing a big picture or context; multisensory resources; kinaesthetic, auditory and visual experiences and the importance of personal motivation.

There are a great variety of approaches to the integration of experiential learning into the curriculum. In centres experiential learning is at the root of the learning process and this methodology should be consistent throughout the early years so that the pathways of learning are consistent and therefore more effective.

'Exploring multiple intelligence through experience and then celebrating through display'

So within our classrooms and centres we need to consider the degree to which we feel able to integrate the above beliefs into our day to day practice. These examples have been collected from across schools in Scotland.

- The adult creates the whole picture for the children at the start of the day, so that children are aware of where the content of the play session fits in.

- The learning is identified in the play opportunity as part of the organisation of resources so that all adults are aware of the purpose.

- Time in the shared play area is well structured and organised with resources and opportunities that fit into identified teaching such as environmental studies programmes, so that all classes can use the same resources with

'Attractive self help areas to increase independence'

a slightly different focus. This allows a greater proportion of the time to be given to play as it can be attributed to percentage allocation times for curriculum.

- Each part of the teaching session in the classroom, involves a balance of oral, written and practical. All aspects of the curriculum are presented in this way so that children who learn in a kinaesthetic way may experience this first and then allow them to make connections when they come to record their thinking. To learn a new concept in a purely receptive way would not be effective for this child.

- Work programmes rotate the groups of children who are with the teacher so that focus time can be given at any point. The focus could be the practical experience rather than the recording if that is seen to be the most effective method of teaching.

- Feedback time is built in to the play experiences through talking and thinking books, general talk sessions, open ended record sheets so that children are aware what they have learnt.

- Play sessions in separate rooms in large schools are timetabled for a whole afternoon/morning. The room is set up with all the areas of play, and the session is set up with clear links across learning. This approach can give a depth of learning since there is a long block of time without interruption although learning from week to week is disjointed.

'Outdoor experiences are shared & valued inside'

- Single classrooms with limited space have play bags/drawers of resources that are used on the table top. Display areas are used to create weekly challenges such as a maths problem, a science investigation, a creative puzzle to develop thinking skills.

- The outdoor area is used by all children in the primary school as another learning environment. Resources are carried out as required although some schools have created zones of play, such as den building, an outdoor classroom, verandas to cover sand and water play, wildlife area and so on. The areas are used at playtimes and during timetabled sessions. Forest schools are developing across Scotland. These outdoor spaces offer children the opportunity to learn in outdoor environments that are natural. The gathering areas are used to provide group focus, opportunities are planned and implemented by the adults who are engaged in the process as 'objective participants'.

In some environments mathematics has been the focus for the active learning approach. The A.L.A.N. (Active Learning Active Numeracy) project started several years ago as a method of creating motivational spaces for numeracy. The approach is based on the attitude that children already have some understanding of maths when they enter school/centres. Observation of some mathematics areas revealed that the resources were often plastic and therefore rather limiting in their potential for sorting. Mathematics had become un-creative and often taught by worksheet.

The range of strategies will be presented in another book called Motivational Mathematics because there are too many to list here. The number line sequence was used many times to encourage children to share their knowledge. The planned progression followed this kind of pathway.

'Displays to stimulate linked activities offered nearby'

- Textured rings to make a line (estimation of number required physical activity to wake up brain).

- Textured balls in a variety of sizes and weights (awareness of size and mass, number counting 1 to 1 tagging).

- Paper slips to record any numbers known (formative assessment, numerical recognition, pictured representation, self esteem of shared deas).

- Paper slips in order (ordinality of number).

- Pipe cleaners to shape into numerals (numerical recognition, manual dexterity).

- Dot cards to match balls in rings (quantity of number).

- Numeral shapes (reinforcement of numeral shape. Exploration of numeral reversal.

As practitioners we should open ourselves to the possibilities of other resources to make learning exciting for young children.

The balance of exposition and exploratory thinking can be biased towards the direct teaching of knowledge /skills/ attitudes related, in this case, to Numeracy. Through the use of initial consultation and a small amount of exposition to present a key point the children were enabled and empowered to share their existing thinking and work together actively to learn. The experience was motivational and open ended enough to offer differentiation through outcome.

In January a group of children had experienced snow and freezing temperatures. The provision of snow flakes to count and white fabrics to explore had provoked the idea of building a Snow Queen's den. Children gathered around a large sheet of paper to share their thinking. Each child had a different colour pen to enable the adult to monitor engagement and contribution. The Talking Tub™ contained a variety of resources that included a tape measure, a thermometer, samples of the fabrics available, photographic images of winter scenes and a variety of housing types. The children handled the materials in order to broaden and deepen the knowledge base. This improved the quality of talking and thinking since they could plan and design with more awareness. The designs and ideas were all accepted, to deepen the mathematical focus the adult used the tape measure to demonstrate its purpose when a child said "I want it this big" and gestured with his hands. The measurements were then recorded by the adult alongside the child's diagram. The degree of adult modelling will obviously alter according to the developmental needs of the children in the group. This experience then flowed into building the den outside, exploring miniature dens in the materials tray, creating two dimensional plans at the dough table and an investigation into snow in the discovery den.

'Explaining ideas for building the Snow Queen's den'

'Applying mathematical knowledge to the shape and dimension of the den'

'A desert of numbers'

If we view the areas of our environments as purely child management then we can begin to focus on the learning that can take place through play and activity. The materials tray offers a sensorial environment for learning. The desert full of numbers will both explore numeral awareness and recognition. The opportunities are motivational and active and are thus able to offer a more appropriate learning opportunity for young children than two dimensional work.

The following grid shows the possibilities of an active, creative learning environment for mathematics and especially numeracy. The zones suggested are the materials tray (sand), water areas, dough (malleable) and the discovery den.

The practical examples below give ideas for the exploration of numeracy.

Materials Tray (Sand)	Water	Malleable	Discovery Den
NMM Level A Magnetic numbers, giant magnet. *Numeral awareness /recognition*	Foam numbers and blindfold. Identify the shape. Try to put them in order. *Number recognition*	Modelling sheet with numeral. Flatten down when finished for whole number shape. *Numeral shape*	Talking and thinking tree. Boxes of different seasonal objects to hang on a branch. Emergent writing onto leaves. Extend with numerals to hang on each branch. *Numeral awareness*
Glitter numbers, 4 baskets, 4 tweezers. *Numeral awareness /recognition*	Fill up capfuls. Variety of scented bottle tops e.g fabric softeners. *Quantity of number*	Make a given number of objects to go in 10 baskets. *Number to 1 matching*	Objects above with pictographic/iconic symbols for quantity. *Quantity of number*
Glitter numbers, tea strainers, box. *Numeral awareness /recognition*	Fill up a dolls tea set with a pipette Match to a number card. *Quantity of number*	A number of characters. make something for each. e.g Sandwhich for a bear 1-1 match	Objects above with numeral hanging on the tree already. *Numeral awareness /recognition*
Glitter numbers, box with a number on top. *Numeral awareness /recognition of quality*	Boats of different sizes. Offcuts of wood and branches to act as cargo *Quantity of number Concept of number size*	Make one.. then share it out between so many characters e.g. 1 cake and five teddies *Fractional sharing Division*	Pipe cleaners. Can you make the shape of a numeral? *Numeral awareness /recognition*
Glitter numbers, box with number word and numeral. *Numeral, word recognition*	Plastic rings, pebbles etc. Objects that are fished out of water and then laid along 'line cards' to aid counting strategies. *L-R counting Tagging objects to count*	Artificial flowers with a few plastic insects. Task cards to make more bugs to visit each flower *Properties of number.*	Brass door numbers inside little pouches so that they can be felt. Can you tell which number is hiding? *Numeral awareness /recognition*
Objects to put into sand to count into a variety of containers. Such as jewels, nuts and bolts, ants, spiders, pom poms, leaves, tickets, soft toys linked to the seasonal theme eg. Hedgehogs in leaves *Conservation and quantity of number*	Variety of frogs and real log sections for them to sit on. *Conservation of number subtratction.*	Offer 2 containers within a context such as two friends and offer 1 cake to share *Division, fractions, subtraction,*	Bags of buttons, gems, spiders, tiny ants etc to feel and estimate how many they think are in the bags... then count etc. *Conservation and quantity of number*
Objects to thread onto yarn to aid counting from left to right in linear form. Beads, pasta tubes, cotton reels, large nuts, large washers, pipe cleaners. *Conservation and quantity of number*	HTU materials hidden in water collect 10 in a box, 10x10 and so on. *Conservation of number Place value and exchange.*	Make three numbers to create new number from dough. *Recognition TU/HTU.*	Cloakroom tickets/old envelopes. *Conservation and quantity of number*

Learning Pathways

Planning For Play - Children's Voices

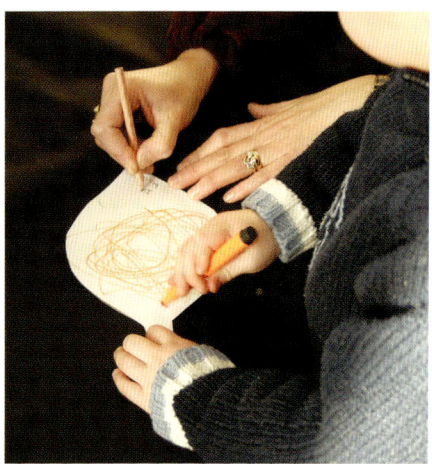

The ideas from children are recorded in Talking & Thinking Floorbooks that can be made for individuals, groups or class.

The features of a Talking and Thinking Book include:

- **Children's ideas and thoughts** without re-framing or interpretation so that they are a genuine record of their thinking. When children give a response to a question or contribute an idea that is far removed from the rest of the group thinking, the idea should be recorded as evidence of contribution, but not engagement.

- **Open ended questions** that are created in response to an interest from the children. The questions are posed as part of a conversation and are designed to stimulate thought rather than test knowledge. The flow of reflective talk is critical to the process, to create a partnership of exploration and discovery. Question and answer sessions create a completely different atmosphere. Questions are almost philosophical, such as I wonder what would happen if..?

- **Higher order thinking.** This level of interest can be stimulated by challenging children to create links in their own learning. Revisiting ideas over long blocks of time support children to see that the process of thinking and learning is full of experimentation and adaptation. The frameworks of understanding that children hold in their brains are created by a wide variety of sensorial input from all the environments they encounter. The Talking and Thinking Books are a method of finding out what they know before, during and after a block of structured experiences.

'Exploring bulbs, batteries & wires'

- **Depth of Learning.** The flow of the book follows children's desire to explore an area in depth. Depth of learning created through giving children time to explore their own thinking is the key to long term embedded knowledge. Collating children's ideas in a book form ensures that the group focus on continuity and progression over longer blocks of time. A discussion that starts within the planning aspect of spring, may focus entirely on how plants know to grow, or what is inside a seed. The rate at which some adult-created, disjointed experiences are presented to children can surely only encourage superficial awareness.

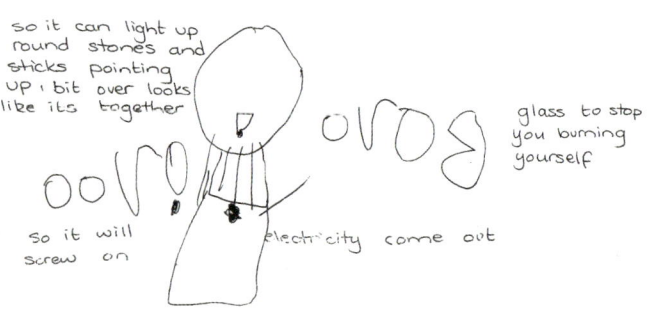

Learning Pathways

- **Collaborative learning.** The books include very large pieces of blank paper that enable children and adults to record their ideas as a group. By giving each person a different coloured marker it is possible to observe who contributes to the group writing. The adult provides a role model for the process of thinking, listening, supporting, suggesting ideas, accepting challenge, being a writer, making diagrams, Mind Maps® to name just a few.

- **A variety of methods of presenting thinking.**
  To respond to different learning styles and preferences the books incorporate a wide range of writing. The adult can scribe for the children to release some from the pressure of secretarial skills during a small group experience; individuals can record their idea in a pictorial form, or writing on a thinking bubble (paper shaped in a thought bubble available freely in writing area) during the play session; photographs or adult observations are included to show the process of exploration and links between children and their learning: The status given to this creates an atmosphere that celebrates the joy of learning. Children will offer challenging questions and become keen to offer ideas and suggestions that are then incorporated into the planning framework.

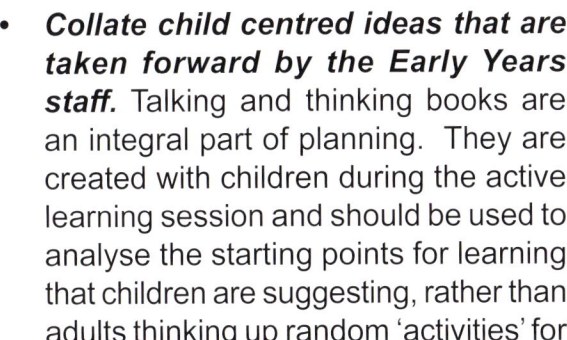

'Thinking about any aspect of the curriculum should be displayed'

- **Collate child centred ideas that are taken forward by the Early Years staff.** Talking and thinking books are an integral part of planning. They are created with children during the active learning session and should be used to analyse the starting points for learning that children are suggesting, rather than adults thinking up random 'activities' for children to 'do'. Responsive planning should be at the root of learning. If we are going to consult children then we should be prepared to change our thinking and actions as a result of it. If the children you are working with have limited oracy then the range of strategies should reflect this, increased observation, use of models, or a 3D mind map are all possibilities.

'Icicles, snowflakes and numbers on the tree'

- **The books are available to children at all times.**
  Joint ownership should give children the right to revisit their thinking whenever they wish. There has to be feedback loop to the children so that they know that the process of consultation is actually changing something. The results of 'meetings' can be recorded, as can voting diagrams and their results. Photographs of physical changes can support this process.

In practice this approach has led to a child centred curriculum, which is based on evidence collated in a child centred way.

When we use this approach of Talking and Thinking Floorbooks™ we can:

- respond to individual intelligences, through our active based experiences.

- enable children to share their own perspectives of a subject that may not have featured in our thinking.

- support the emotional development of the children through affirmation, by valuing what they think and offer to us.

- understand the need that some children have for varying degrees of structure and order in their play, and the way that we can support them through resources, time, space and adult interaction.

'Creative environments enable children to explore & experiment'

'Measurement with a real purpose'

- use a methodology that responds to the learning styles, so that the play becomes more closely matched to the needs and desires of the children.

- begin to understand the opportunities that will motivate children to challenge themselves through taking on board their ideas and consulting them in the process.

- enable the feedback loop of meta-cognition to reach the children so that observation, discussion, recording and planning are in a continuous path that integrates the child as an individual, rather than in a line away from the child towards too much adult direction.

- create challenging opportunities for adults and children to think. The collaboration between children and adults raises the potential for learning.

- Link together different aspects of their understanding to create a holistic learning environment.

So when all the elements are put together it is apparent that children are engaged in learning in a creative way. This is the stuff of childhood, a place of awe and wonderment that should be celebrated throughout the educational process.

'Mathematics through an interest in rats!'

Assessment for Learning

Assessment - The Role Of The Adult In Gathering Information

It is generally agreed that the most effective way for adults to gather information about young children and their thinking is to observe what the children are doing; listen to what they say in order to deepen the picture; question to challenge their thinking in order to unravel frameworks of understanding; reflect and review; and then offer more challenges to stretch or consolidate the learning.

'Ideas on the 'Talking & Thinking' Tree'

Assessment should be an integral part of learning and teaching. Without it the match between what we provide and what children need to challenge them would be too great. In an experiential approach to learning the formalized recording that leads to assessment is often inappropriate due to the nature of play. The solutions to this must lie in alternative methods of gathering information. Observation, consultation through talking and listening and strategies that encourage self assessment and reflection such as mind maps. Talking & Thinking Floorbooks™ can be used as class group or individual 'play diaries' to celebrate the process of active learning.

Observation

Many adults still feel unsure about the time given to observation, yet without effective observation the provision may not match the needs of the children. The closer the match between the perceived need (what we think they need) and the actual need (what they actually need) the more effective the learning will be.

'Adult enjoyment of children learning'

There are two main types of observation:

Focused Observation: Children are identified for a number of different reasons e.g. they could be at a key learning point, or are perhaps not progressing. A structured approach, accompanying aide memoir and descriptive form usually support photographic, video or audio evidence.

Informal Observation: Observations are made by the staff whilst interacting/observing during the general play session. Notes are made in either the areas of play or centrally and are collated at a later date to include in records or to inform the responsive planning.

Wood and Atfield (1996) suggest that practitioners need to "liberate themselves from the guilt of standing back and observing". Many practitioners would maintain that they are always observing, but not through standing back. The evidence to support the time given to an adult looking without interruption can be gained most effectively through trying it. All people make assumptions, and create subjective impressions. The skill for the adult carrying out an observation is to describe exactly what they see and hear. Hughes (1986) identifies an issue linked to the observation of numeracy, where the key worker is the adult most able to observe and identify the child's frameworks of understanding and may not necessarily be located in the vicinity of the child.

Observations are only really of use if they are analysed, so that their meaning and relevance can be discussed with the whole Early Years team. Interpretations of the observations should be challenged or validated by all the adults in the centre, since personalities and preferences will affect the way the child interacts or plays.

Drummond (1993) suggests that assessment should be part of an act of understanding and that, rather than being confined to what the children say and do, it should be informed by deeper questions and a broader vision.

'Assessment of P3 mathematics programme on the Talking & Thinking Tree'

The need to track evidence of learning across a variety of activities can be used to check how the child is using, applying and transferring knowledge and skills in a variety of contexts. The tracking observations are particularly relevant for the identification of repeatable behaviours (schema), where the learning links are clear if children are encouraged to move between areas of play. Tracking is also often carried out over a period of time to help adults understand patterns of learning and ongoing cognitive concerns.

One of the problems encountered when assessing children's learning through activity, is that it is often difficult to be sure whether the play activity itself has stimulated new learning, whether it is providing a context for mastery and revision, or whether it enables children to reveal what they already know, can do and understand. Wood and Attfield (1996) suggest that there are no easy answers to this challenge, apart from the use of sensitive interactions from adults, careful observation and a framework for discussing observations.

Time should be spent on the creation of a common, coherent, shared framework for observation and assessment, so that the process is easier and more meaningful and can provide the evidence on which to base further planning. The Talking and Thinking Floorbook™ provides baseline understanding as formative assessment through the recording of adult observation and children's voices. A summative assessment takes place at the end of the experiences to reflect on what has been learnt.

'Consulting children inside & out to aid assessment from 2 to 18 years'

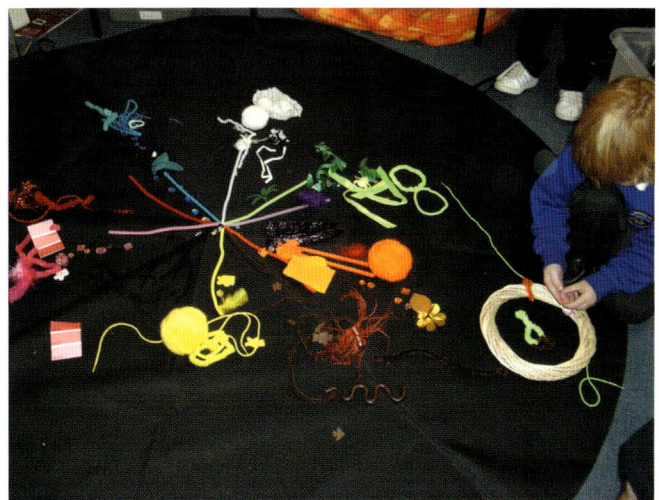
'Colour sorting by shade/tone'

Consultation With Children

When the opportunity to involve children in the process of learning occurs, it is much easier to assess their existing frameworks of understanding in any aspect of the curriculum. The long term assimilation of knowledge, skills and attitudes into practical experiences is the demonstration of deeper understanding. Children have a great deal to share and should be consulted through planning together, focused discussion and methods laid out below. Self-reflection gives a better feedback loop, since the learner needs to acknowledge what they are having difficulty with before they move on.

Recording Thinking

We all have a variety of learning styles and therefore more appropriate ways of recording and thinking about learning. Play is a creative process and lends itself to forms of recording that are more open ended than many staff feel comfortable with. As a group of professionals we need to have a healthy debate about the purpose of written recording of learning. Is the evidence collated *really* evidence of assimilation and accommodation?

'Annotated mark making on leaves'

Mind maps encourage children to see the links across learning (Buzan 2004), to place learning into contexts that give us an emotional link to learning that should enable our brains to retain information more effectively.

Talking and thinking Floorbooks™ (Warden 2004) are records of the process of learning. They record childrens thinking through their speech, diagrams, 3D mind maps, photographs, emergent writing and pictures. The whole emphasis is on children finding a variety of ways of sharing their

'Observations by adult put onto tree'

knowledge. In the early stages talking and thinking books are created as part of a group, the more able children use individual talking and thinking books. Children are taught a variety of methods of recording their thinking. These books enable adults to assess children's learning when they have been working independently.

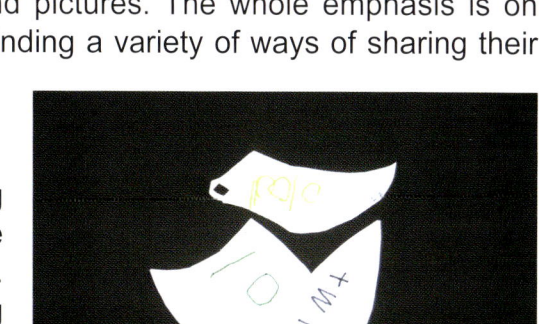
'Child's own writing'

These pages help our team clarify how we view assessment. Discussions within individual staff teams and Education Authorities regarding the way they wish to collate and use activity based assessment will undoubtedly affect strategies and layout. 'Assessment is for learning' have created a diagram to demonstrate their links. We have incorporated our strategies to show the place of activity based assessment.

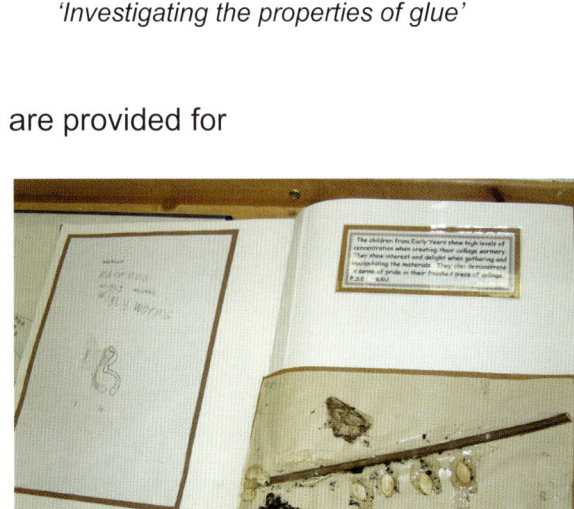

'Investigating the properties of glue'

Why do we assess?

- to inform planning
- to identify individual strengths and needs
- to ensure that individual needs and interests are provided for
- to ensure continuity and progression
- to encourage staff to reflect on practice
- to identify next steps in learning for staff and children to provide a picture of the child's all round development for parents, children and staff

Who shares the assessment?

'Demonstrating understanding through oracy, creativity and diagrams'

- children
- parent/carers
- staff working with children
- staff at the previous and nextstage
- other relevant professionals
- external partners e.g. partner provider centre, wrap around care settings, out-of-school care provision

How will our assessment affect what we do?

- improve attainment and achievement
- develop skills and competency
- increase interactions with adults and peers
- increase progression
- encourage use of personal learning plans
- encourage independence
- increase interest and motivation
- encourage involvement of stakeholders
- demonstrate an understanding of agreed focus
- broaden the balance and breadth of experience
- increase effectiveness of learning environment
- grow knowledge and understanding
- incorporate use of prior information such as the transition record and other data on children

Nathen and Adrianna support each other when trying to measure their worm's. whilst measuring their worm it was *stretched* a little too far. Nathen held both ends up and said "Now I have two worms" ie worms were then measured separately then put back ir the wormery to re-build it's self.

How can we assess?

- observation in a range of situations - tracking and single
- minutes of meetings with children
- formal plans
- discussions with staff, parents, carers.
- samples of children's work
- check lists or schedules
- notebooks
- sampling techniques
- involving children in self-evaluation
- audio visual materials
- class lists
- target setting information
- evaluations
- use of other data e.g. national test data

Who collects?

- children self evaluation/selection
- parents e.g. feedback books
- teachers e.g. recorded information
- nursery nurses e.g. talking/listening
- students
- auxilliaries
- classroom assistance
- headteachers/managers
- childcare workers
- training and care assistants
- LEA staff, including
    - Early Intervention Core Team
    - Childcare Core Team
    - other professionals
- Service managers
- others as appropriate

How will our assessments be used?

- to inform planning and organisation
- to focus on specific aspects of the curriculum and of the child's learning
- to ensure breadth, balance, continuity and progression
- to improve practice and provision
- to evaluate learning and teaching
- to contribute towards a profile and understanding in the individual child
- to help develop partnership to reflect on their own learning
- to provide information for other professionals
- to pass information to the next stage

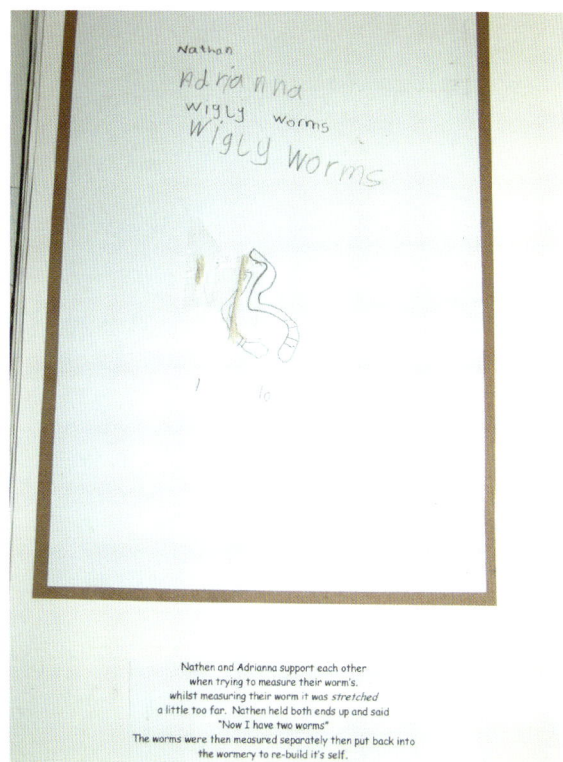

'Diagram with writing support'

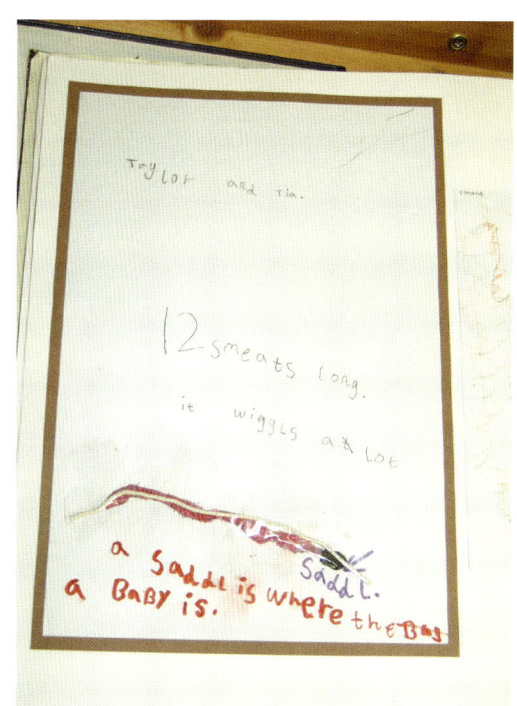

'Extending thinking across curriculum boundaries'

Resources

- Play diaries
- Learning logs
- Learning wall to chart the developments and experiences for children over a block of time.
- Consultation boards both inside and outside
- Draft books - low grade paper to minimise implicit pressure to use secretarial skills\ Talking & Thinking Floorbooks™
- Transition records
- Codes of practice from Council and external partner organisations
- Council planning formats
- The Child at the Centre
- 3-5/5-14 Curriculum Framework/Curriculum for Excellence
- Personal learning plans and grids

'Exploration and ideas at the beginning and end of investigation recorded to share with a wider audience'

'Recording using a play diary'

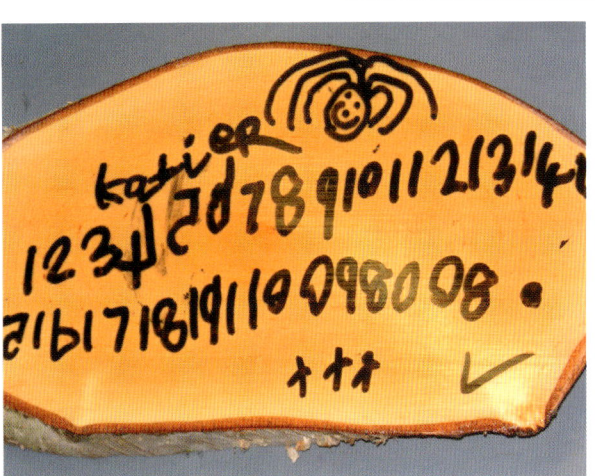

'Recording ideas in creative ways - writing on wood'

'Consultation board'

The assessment triangle featured on the opposite page highlights the integration of assessment as a tool for learning, assessment to make teaching and learning more effective and assessment of the process of children's learning. The areas in red are used to visually demonstrate the way that our approach and strategies integrate into the wider framework. Some staff are still using formalised assessment procedures as summative tasks until they feel more confident that attainment will take place in a more active child-centred space. It is hoped that over time these forms of assessment will be adjusted.

Creating A Place Where Everyone Is Learning Together

Our pupils and staff identify and reflect on their own evidence of learning.

- Journal writing.
- Play diaries.
- Increased oracy.
- Learning walls.

Our pupils and staff help to set their own goals.

- High scope plans.
- P.L. plans.
- Talking & Thinking Floorbooks™ used as discussion focus.

Our pupils and staff practise self- and peer-assessment.

- Group Talking & Thinking Floorbooks™
- Individual thinking books as a focus for discussion.

Curriculum

ASSESSMENT **AS**

Learning and Teaching

Staff use a range of evidence from day-to-day activities to check on pupil's progress.

- Photographic sequences.
- Consultation boards.
- Draft books/diaries.

ASSESSMENT **OF**

ASSESSMENT **FOR**

Our pupils, staff and parents are clear about what is to be learned and what success would be like.

- Shared focus.
- Learning stories.
- Home/school diaries.

Assessment

Staff talk and work together to share standards in and across schools.

Staff talk and work together to share standards in an across schools.

- Talking & Thinking Floorbooks™ to evaluate quality of provision.

Staff use assessment information to monitor their establishment's provision and progress, and to plan for improvement

- Evidence collated in floorbooks
- Learning stories
- Play diaries.

Our pupils and staff are fully involved in deciding next steps in their learning and identifying who can help

- Clear links between floorbooks, learning stories & P.L. plans.

Our classroom assessment involves high quality interactions, based on thoughtful questioning, careful listening and reflective responses

- Increased time to discuss and hypothesise.
- Exploration and investigation in active play.

Learning Pathways 51

Activity Zones

There are many ways of organising play and the nature of play is such that it will be cross-curricular. The zone is used as an organisational tool to support children in their play. Associated resources are stored effectively nearby and the position of dividers seems to support children to engage in the learning. This section of the book will look at good practice in the organisation and presentation of the environment. We have selected five zones to focus on in the primary school in order to make the organisation more attainable. It is of note that the areas should be seen to be flexible and that any curricular area can be delivered in any zone. The actual opportunities that take place in these zones are bound to be structured in some way by the adult. It is hoped that practitioners will take on board the Talking & Thinking Floorbooks™ approach in order to raise the level of consultation with children.

The zones are:

Role Play. This zone can actually overtake and influence all the other opportunities taking place within the learning environment since it is highly motivational. The storyline approach weaves together the whole curriculum in a purposeful way.

Discovery Den. This zone is designed to raise the profile of science and technology as a playful experience. It links to the concept that children have existing frameworks of understanding to help them make sense of the world. It is a zone of enquiry and investigation, of hypothesis and thinking.

Outdoor Learning. Children need to be active outside and for some children it is the optimal learning zone. With appropriate clothing it can be used throughout the year. Forest Schools and outdoor classrooms have become embedded practice in many parts of the country.

Materials Tray. Children are sensorial learners and should therefore be given access to textural materials in a variety of ways. Water and sand are just the beginning of this pathway. We can use the materials zone to apply and consolidate any area of the curriculum through changing the small scale resources we provide.

Small World/Construction. The construction zone can be creative and dynamic when it is resourced effectively. The provision of smaller items gives a more imaginative focus that engages children in a complimentary way. Creative, abstract blocks combined with fabrics open up an endless range of possibilities.

The following pages will explore each of these areas and start the process of discussion and reflection on the way each school/centre wishes to operate.

The Learning Pathways file provides a more detailed framework to support staff if required. Play and experiential learning cannot be over directed or they will lose the nature that makes them such effective teaching and learning tools. HMIE are exploring the phrase "rich" experiences to support staff to take ownership of the learning rather than implant an over-structured system onto children. Our approach would support this, the Learning Pathways is a framework which can provide some structure at the start of the process to enable staff to move away from high structure to a more flexible open-ended methodology.

Role Play

The Greek word for drama means 'living through' and the action of the drama needs to be lived through by players using 'make-believe' to create the setting for their pretend existence.

In order to make this development framework effective it is necessary to define the authors understanding and interpretation of dramatic play beyond simply 'make believe'.

Why is drama important in the early years?

The degree of involvement and type of role-play alters with the stage and development of the children's play. It is significant in the development of early language. Where drama and role-play were used *effectively* there appeared to be better overall standards in literacy due to the rich experiences that the zone provides.

Dramatic play can actually enhance all areas of the curriculum. Children can set the agenda and learn about things that interest them. It is a method of learning that allows the children and teacher to function as equals/ change roles. What children do and say can be challenged, questioned and analysed by the children themselves. It encourages children to hold two worlds in their heads at the same time.

'Child and adult labelling'

What is dramatic play?

Let us first look at the difference between socio-dramatic play and dramatic play. Klugman and Smilansky (1990) make the distinction in terms of the interaction that occurs during play. When a child believes 'as if' he/she is someone else then the child is involved in dramatic play. If the child interacts with at least one other child (or adult) while pretending, then their play is becoming socio-dramatic. So in an early years environment both tend to occur at various points during the session. For ease of reading the author will refer to both experiences under the umbrella of dramatic play.

When asked the question, 'What is dramatic play?' many practitioners see the two terms in the same way, with a tendency to focus on socio-dramatic play for social interaction. Practitioners include such things as puppetry, small world, structured drama sessions in the hall, responding to stories and books, storytelling, dressing up, fantasy play, adult direction tapes, and expression games.

There have been a number of different terms used over the years and I certainly believe that all of the things above can feed into a dramatic play situation. However there are two main areas of dramatic play that help us to define and organise the lists a little better.

A) Role play is the action of taking on board a role of anything from an inanimate chair, to a dog, to a king. Children have ownership of who they wish to become and for what length of time. Storylines and ideas are often created by the group and all enter into an agreement of sustained disbelief, even though they know that they are clearly in reality. Within this broad band there is role play that often happens in an area and fantasy play that can happen in any space, with anyone, for any length of time. The free and highly responsive aspects of fantasy play are valuable within dramatic play but are difficult to use as the basis for 'educational drama' which tends to be socio-dramatic.

B) Dramatisation is far more structured or directed. Adults/books/stories give a clear pathway for the children to follow. The depth of emotion felt by the children can be superficial since they become directed to behave in certain ways to 'look the part' e.g. A smiley face does not necessarily connect with an internal emotion of happiness. Dramatisation often leads to 'performance art' which many theorists see as being more appropriate to children in the later stages of the primary school, Some children enjoy the experience of being watched so that there is an atmosphere of performance. However these 'shows' are created by the children from their dramatic play and evolve and change with every performance. There are examples of possibilities given for festivals and celebrations that are more child centred and less stressful for the children and the adults that work with them.

'Real resources to reflect reality therefore increasing the quality of learning'

The middle path lies within role play where an underlying scaffolding of structure combines with adult ideas to meet objectives and curriculum demands. The actual context for the area is left to the children, the next step is to enable children to have ownership of their area through planning and building it, moving to the play during the session, the adult has a definite role to keep the sense of drama or dramatic tension going through the introduction of scenarios, storytelling, additional props etc in response to the observations made in the area. When the play has moved on and the children have transformed and developed the area as far as they wish to go then a period of reflection can be quite worthwhile to evaluate the effectiveness of the play. These stages were referred to by Nisbet (1986) as Getting started, Keeping Going, and Looking Back.

The approach that we take to role play is called the storyline approach, which is outlined on the following pages. Children are motivated by an initial start point. Ideas and suggestions are collated through the Talking & Thinking Floorbooks™ . Some of the ideas will become the framework of planning for the active learning experiences. The decision is made based on curricular focus, whether the idea is achievable and the group consensus. Some of the resources can be made and this provides the most learning potential, others should be provided to create a rich environment. It is not enough to put plastic food on a table and call it a shop! The final stage of the role play process is closure and should be done with the children not by the adult after the children have all gone home. (Warden 2001)

Storyline Guide Sheet

1. Starting Points
Ideas to start the role play off.

The type of role play area should be guided by observations made within the classroom/centre. The ideas included in this section are taken from children who have initiated dramatic play themselves or from adult generated planning. The purpose is to create motivational and appropriate contexts that will encourage children to develop the role play area themselves.

2. Resources
Resources to make and obtain.

The success behind every role play area depends upon the resources available. Ideally you should have a large number of resources in stock from which you can select items, when appropriate. At the beginning of the session there should be plenty of space for the children to move, which will enable them to design and create their own layout. Too many items at this stage of play will inhibit their ability to step into imaginary play. Children should be supported in the creation of their own resources by using multi sensory materials rather than plastic pre-made products.

3. Scenarios
Events.

The quality of many dramatic play areas drops away after a short time because the potential of the area has been explored by the children. To reflect real life, the introduction of events will maintain children's motivation and interest, therefore learning will follow. This section contains possible scenarios and items to include in a role play bag that will improve the quality of play and hopefully deepen the child's knowledge and understanding of the world around them.

4. Closures
Bringing the role play to a close.

When children have been involved in dramatic play through the creation of a role play area they will have developed a sense of involvement. To finish a context by simply removing the area does not allow children the opportunity to bring their storyline/play to an end. The closure of a role play area usually presents itself at some point within the play, following observation of the children. A few ideas have been included as examples from practice.

The Vets

1. Starting Points
Ideas to start the role play off.

An injured animal arrives with a letter from a passer-by asking the children in the centre to help.

A child comes in with a 'hurt' animal.

The letter arrives from the vet saying he is ill, and can the children take over until he/she gets better.

Pet Rescue are full up, can the children help to home some pets.

2. Resources
Resources to make and obtain.

Beds/cages (from cardboard boxes)
Animals
Syringes/medicines/dried food
Bandages
Charts for temperature
Phone/clock/scales
Notepad
Appointment pad
Posters
Information books (made by children)
White coat/gloves/thermometer
Pet cages/newspaper/water bottles/food bowls/poo tray!
Shelving (created with large blocks) An animal dies.

Combine this page with the ideas from the 'children's planning sheet' (on CD).

3. Scenarios
Events.

More animals arrive throughout the time, to stimulate functional reading to find out what their needs are. Linked book & toy animal.

Children enter the room to discover that an animal has escaped. Torches, map, mobile phone, cage.

The animals need feeding. Measure jugs, dried foods, containers.

Animal returns to good health.

4. Closures
Bringing the role play to a close.

The animal dies!

Vet returns.

Someone comes to claim their pet and leaves a thank you note.

Learning Pathways

Discovery Den

The Discovery Den is a place of exploration and thinking where children are encouraged to think and process their ideas in any aspect of the curriculum. The underlying approach is one of enquiry so science and mathematical challenges are the easiest to create. The 'den' environment is one that encourages children to settle and engage in the opportunity. Drapes hung overhead have an effect on the environment, it has an enclosed feel so that children feel they are entering a special space to explore. The transparent nets do allow children to watch each other as they approach the same challenge in a different way. This leads children to have wonderful conversations about approaches and techniques in learning. (Warden 2006)

My approach has two elements with the underpinning approach of explore, talk, think and explore some more required.

- The first is to offer open ended challenges related to a context. Such as 'A dog has three biscuits and 5 bowls how will he share them out?' The discovery area then offers real materials to work with metal bowls, a furry dog and a dough bone to divide. The solution and more importantly the thinking behind them is shared with the group or class.
- The second is to create Bags of Discovery that are wide and varied in their content so that children can see how everyday things are connected. We have bags of everyday, real objects to sort and classify such as spoons or to explore concepts such as light. The children are able to sort and classify in ways that make sense to them and show this thinking through the Talking and Thinking Floorbooks™ or individual books that have mind map cues and shapes to support the recording of ideas.

'Discovery den to offer investigations'

Explore

Hands on experiences are crucial to children. The richness of some environments are limited due to the use of too many plastic resources, the sets should be made from real materials, some of which will need to be handled with care. The complete bags have been designed for adult/child time, however some of the tools of investigation should also be available freely through the play session. Materials are at hand to aid investigation.

Talk

The talk that takes place is of paramount importance and should therefore be recorded in some way, so that it influences the subsequent learning opportunities. I use a Talking and Thinking Floorbook™ that records children's ideas (frameworks of understanding) through recorded talk, children's pictures, mind maps, and the process of discovery through photographs. All of the ideas children suggest should be included in the book. It is a celebration of thinking not 'correct answers'.

Think

The children can revisit the book to add more ideas, or disagree with their earlier ones. The book approach enables practitioners, parents and children to see the development of scientific thought over

'Mirrors can be used to change perspective'

time. Children have clear ideas about the world they live in, by talking to children about their own ideas it enables the practitioners the opportunity to create child centred opportunities. This method consults children and gives them ownership of the play process whilst still creating an adult framework. Their ideas can then be integrated into the opportunities.

And Explore Some More

The blend of adult and child interaction is very important if children are going to feel able to investigate and explore freely. The ethos of the environment they are in should support them to take risks, get things wrong, and then persevere with another line of enquiry.

The learning opportunities, that accompany a Bag of Discovery, are many and varied. These resources should be readily available, in labelled containers, so that the practitioner can locate them easily and therefore respond to the children.

Additional resources to use in investigative opportunities:

'Creating an investigative space'

Colour

Range of objects in different shades.
Materials to create objects in a variety of colours (modelling clay).
Coloured perspex.
Mirrors to look through and in.

Pattern

Create pattern cards (black and yellow).
Sheets of fabrics to compare on A6 boards
Colour charts (from paint samples)

Magnification

Sheet magnifiers
Sheet minimizers
Optic wonder
Wooden magnifier
Binoculars
Materials with a variety of magnification (x2, x10)

Light Diffraction
(by looking at objects through viewer)

Diffraction lens
Fly's eye sheet
Overhead projector

'Supporting design and investigation through literacy'

Materials (wood, metal, plastic, rubber)

Examples of the raw material e.g. piece of wood
Examples of different objects made in same materials. e.g. wooden spoon
Provide magnets to explore which materials are magnetic.

Measure (length)

Different types and styles of measuring tape.
Dressmaking, linear, imperial, metric

Measure (mass)

Balance scales
Real objects to weigh

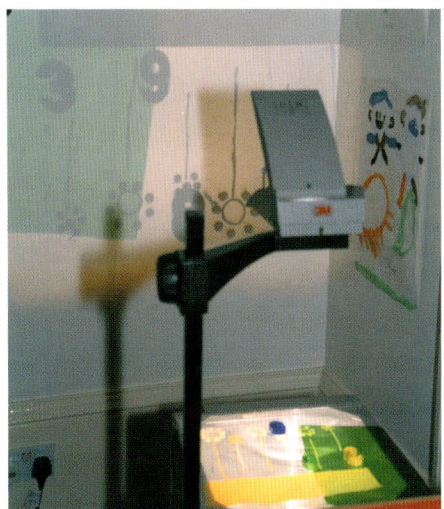
'Use of OHP's to create investigations into light and opacity'

Measure (dimensions)

Different types and styles of measuring tape.
Measuring compass
Sliding rule with measuring prong

Buoyancy

Transparent tank to explore floating and sinking

Magnetism

Bar magnet to define polarity
Variety of magnets to test magnetism
Magnets of varying strengths and shapes

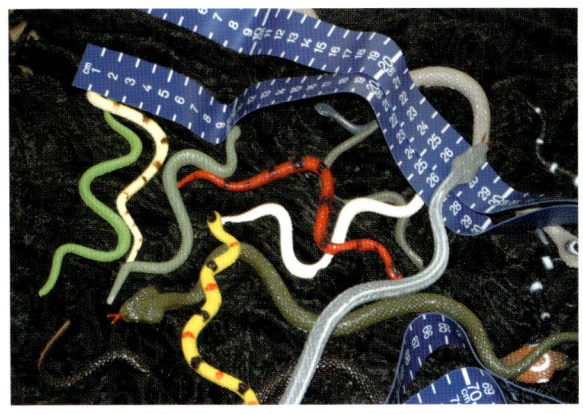
'Measurement in context'

Learning In Outdoor Spaces

All children need access to an outdoor area. The style of an outdoor area varies considerably between centres and schools. The Curriculum for Excellence states very clearly that some of the learning should take place outside. Schools have explored the possibilities of an outdoor classroom, waterproofs for children and adults and some have re-written curriculum plans so that they can be delivered outside. Early years centres should have prolonged and daily access to outdoor play. This section highlights the vision that we hold for outdoor learning. (Warden 2005)

- **Young children should be outdoors as much as indoors and need a well-designed, well-organised, integrated indoor-outdoor environment, preferably with indoors and outdoors available simultaneously.**

Outdoor provision is an essential part of the child's daily environment and life, not an option or an extra. Each half of the indoor-outdoor environment offers significantly different, but complementary, experiences and ways of being to young children. They should be available simultaneously and be experienced in a joined-up way, with each being given equal status and attention for their contribution to young children's well-being, health, stimulation and all areas of development.

Outdoor space must be considered a necessary part of a school based early years environment, be well thought through and well organised to maximise its value and usability by children and adults, and design and planning must support developmentally appropriate practice, being driven by children's interests and needs.

'Creating structures in clay and wood'

- **Play is the most important activity for young children outside.**

Play is the means through which children find stimulation, well-being and happiness, and is the means through which they grow physically, intellectually and emotionally. Play is the most important thing for children to do outside and the most relevant way of offering learning outdoors. The outdoor environment is very well suited to meeting children's needs for all types of play, building upon first-hand experiences.

- **Outdoor provision can, and must, offer young children experiences which have a lot of meaning to them and are led by the child.**

Because of the freedom the outdoors offers to move on a large scale, to be active, noisy and messy and to use all their senses with

'Art - through making own clay & charcoal outside'

their whole body, young children engage in the way they most need to explore, make sense of life and express their feeling and ideas. Many young children relate much more strongly to learning offered outdoors rather than indoors.

All areas of learning must be offered through a wide range of holistic experiences, both active and calm, which make the most of what the outdoors has to offer.

Outdoor provision needs to be organised so that children are stimulated and able to follow their own interests and needs through play-based activity, giving them independence, self-organisation, participation and empowerment. The adult role is crucial in achieving this effectively.

'Creativity & movement on an outdoor stage'

- **Young children need all the adults around them to understand why outdoor play provision is essential for them, and adults who are committed and able to make its potential available to them.**

Children need practitioners who value and enjoy the outdoors themselves, see the potential and consequences it has for young children's well-being and development, and want to be outside with them. Attitude, understanding, commitment and positive thinking are important, as well as the skills to make the best use of what the outdoors has to offer and to effectively support child-led learning; the adult role outdoors must be as deeply considered as that indoors. Practitioners must be able to recognise, capture and share children's learning outdoors with parents and other people working with the child, so that they too become enthused. Cultural differences in attitude to the outdoors need to be understood and worked with sensitively to reach the best outcomes for children.

- **The outdoor space and curriculum must harness the special nature of the outdoors, to offer children what the indoors cannot. This should be the focus for outdoor provision, complementing and extending provision indoors.**

'Technology in creating tunnels & passages'

The outdoors offers young children essential experiences vital to their well-being, health and development in all areas. Children who miss these experiences are significantly deprived.

Outdoors, children can have the freedom to explore different ways of 'being', feeling, behaving and interacting; they have space - physical (up as well as sideways), mental and emotional; they have room and permission to be active, interactive, messy, noisy and work on a large scale; they may feel less controlled by adults.

The real contact with the elements, seasons and the natural world, the range of perspectives, sensations and environments - multi-dimensional and multi-sensory, and the daily change, uncertainty, surprise and excitement all contribute to the desire young children have to be outside. It cannot be the same indoors, a child cannot *be* the same indoors - outdoors is a vital, special and deeply engaging place for young children.

- **Outdoors should be a dynamic, flexible and versatile place where children can choose, create, change and be in charge of their play environment.**

Outdoor provision can, and should, offer young children an endlessly versatile, changeable and responsive environment for all types of play where they can manipulate, create, control and modify. This offers a huge sense of freedom, which is not readily available indoors. It also underpins the development of creativity and the dispositions for learning. The space itself as well as resources, layout, planning and routines all need to be versatile, open-ended and flexible to maximise their value to the child.

- **Young children must have a rich outdoor environment full of irresistible stimuli, contexts for play, exploration and talk, plenty of real experiences and contact with the natural world and with the community.**

Through outdoor play, young children can learn the skills of social interaction and friendship, care for living things and their environment, be curious and fascinated, experience awe, wonder and joy and become 'lost in the experience'. They can satisfy their deep urge to explore, experiment and understand and become aware of their community and locality, thus developing a sense of connection to the physical, natural and human world.

'Movable materials'

A particular strength of outdoor provision is that it offers children many opportunities to experience the real world, have first-hand experiences, do real tasks and do what adults do, including being involved in the care of the outdoor space. Settings should make the most of this aspect, with connected play opportunities.

An aesthetic awareness of and emotional link to the non-constructed or controlled, multi-sensory and multi-dimensional natural world is a crucial component of human well-being, and increasingly absent in young children's lives. The richness of cultural diversity is an important part of our everyday world; this can and should be explored by children through outdoor experiences. Giving children a sense of belonging to something bigger than the immediate family or setting lays foundations for living as a community within the school and beyond.

- **Young children should have long periods of time outside. They need to know that they can be outside every day, when they want to and that they can develop their ideas for play over time.**

High quality play outdoors, where children are deeply involved, only emerges when they know they are not hurried. They need to have time to develop their use of spaces and resources and uninterrupted time to develop their play ideas, or to construct a place and then play in it or to get into problem-solving on a big scale. They need to be able to return to projects again and again until 'finished' with them.

'Sectioned table for transient art'

Slow learning is good learning, giving time for assimilation. When children can move between indoors and outside, their play or explorations develop further still. Young children also need time (and places) to daydream, look on or simply relax outside.

Young children need challenge and risk within a framework of security and safety. The outdoor environment lends itself to offering challenge, helping children learn how to be safe and to be aware of others.

Children are seriously disadvantaged if they do not learn how to approach and manage physical and emotional risk. They can become either timid or reckless, or be unable to cope with consequences. Young children need to be able to set and meet their own challenges, become aware of their limits and push their abilities (at their own pace), be prepared to make mistakes, and experience the pleasure of feeling capable and competent. Challenge and its associated risk are vital for this. Young children also need to learn how to recognise and manage risk as life-skills, so as to become able to act safely, for themselves and others.

'Construction areas in the outdoor space'

Safety of young children outdoors is paramount and a culture of 'risk assessment to enable' that permeates every aspect of outdoor provision is vital for all settings. Young children also need to feel secure, nurtured and valued outdoors. This includes clear behavioural boundaries (using rules to enable freedom), nurturing places and times outside and respect for how individual children prefer to play and learn.

- **Outdoor provision must support inclusion and meet the needs of individuals, offering a diverse range of play-based experiences. Young children should participate in decisions and actions affecting their outdoor play.**

Provision for learning outdoors is responsive to the needs of very active learners, those who need sensory or language stimulation and those who need space away from others – it makes provision more inclusive and is a vital learning environment. When children's learning styles are valued, their self-image benefits. Boys, who tend to use active learning modes more than girls and until they are older, are particularly disadvantaged by limited outdoor play.

All children need full access to provision outdoors and it is important to know and meet the needs and interests of each child as an individual. Young children react differently to the spaces and experiences available or

'Physical development in climbing'

Learning Pathways 63

created so awareness and flexibility are key to the adult role. Observation and assessment (formative and summative), and intervention for particular support, must be carried out outside. While it is important to ensure the safety of all children, it is equally important to ensure all are sufficiently challenged.

The outdoor area is an area that can engage children in all aspects of the curriculum – the science outcome that relates to the 'vastness of the sky and the stars within it' cannot be achieved without going outside in the dark. Unfortunately in some areas the light pollution is so great that young children cannot see the stars.

The Eco-school programme fits in hand in hand with the four capacities that underpin the Curriculum for Excellence. Children are closely connected to Nature and many are leading the way to develop environmental aspects of both the inside and the outside space.

'Growing and composting'

'Photographic support to stimulate play'

Many educational sites do not have a landscaped environment that has been created for outdoor learning. The wonder of children is that with minimal efforts to provide outdoor clothing, some shelter and natural elements, learning can and does happen.

Young children should take an active part in decisions and actions for outdoor provision, big and small. Their perspectives and views are critical and must be sought, and they can take an active role in setting up, clearing away and caring for the outdoor space.

Materials Tray

The materials tray is the title of the zone of resources that encompass the sand and water tray. The location of the materials tray can be small or large and in a variety of storage boxes. The nature of some areas is that they do not have the space to create large sand areas and the same in water. This book has focused on the more unusual ways of using the materials tray so that practitioners see the potential of the space for teaching and learning.

Possibilities include:

- Tuff trays (group work)
- Potting trays (individual/pair work)
- Dog baskets with no holes in the base (individual/pair work)
- Trays with deep and shallow recesses (to explore depth)
- Gravel trays/ Grow bag trays for greenhouses (small group)
- Large mat on the floor (outdoor)
- Paddling pools for group play (outdoor)
- Titchy Tubs that can be adjusted for height and location to be linear, square and individual spaces (very flexible) Can be used at the end of a table to provide 'handling space' next to a tray.
- Provision of plastic mirror and a small amount of resource can give the illusion of quantity

'Small scale experiences to widen opportunities'

The term 'materials tray' suggests a greater range of opportunities than those usually associated with the sand tray. The emphasis in our work is that it represents a space where children can encounter sensorial materials.

Materials that could be used include:

- Sand wet and dry
- Sand soaked with water leaving pools of water on the top
- Silver sand
- Grit
- Pebbles
- Stones and gravel
- Leaves
- Grass turf
- Water
- Mud
- Shells
- Coloured sand
- Gloop!!
- Large wood shavings

'Variety of sensorial materials'

Learning Pathways

Water

The water tray is of the same importance since it can be used in so many different ways. The container for the water will influence the management of it. Non slip matting, open mesh and micro-cloths all reduce the slipping hazard when water is used inside. The water zone will be easier to manage in a tuff tray or shallow potting tray on the table since the water involved is minimal and the amount used considerable reduced. The potting trays have shelves above that can be used for simple storage of resources that are being used in the focus.

There should be a progression through the experiences from 3-8 years old. Changing the container from shallow to deep or deep to variable is one of the ways it can be achieved.

A water zone should provide:

- Two trays with guttering channel between them to explore the movement of water.
- One tray, with smaller containers within, to explore capacity.
- Materials that allow changes in texture such as essential oils, corn flour, ice cubes.
- Small buckets.
- Pipettes, basters, syringes for transporting water.
- Plastic bottles with a variety of shapes and openings to extend accuracy and hand and eye co-ordination.
- Miniature plastic bottles, tiny funnels and small jugs increase the challenge.
- Sponges in a variety of sizes, shapes and types to explore absorbency.
- See through containers-rigid and flexible to explore conservation of shape.
- Flexible rubber tubing in a variety of diameters for syphons.
- Small mirrors that enables children to look at flow and pattern of water.
- Clipboard and paper for recording - laminated grids and chinagraph.

'Water trays should be different as children get older to create an extension in their experiences'

'Tiny water set'

One effective way to structure water play is to put together bags or containers of materials used to explore scientific concepts such as absorbency, nature of water, jets and water pressure and capacity.

Absorbency: sponges in a variety of sizes of waterproof fabrics, soak-up cloths, flannel pieces, containers to measure water.

Nature of Water: materials to absorb/repel, trickle over, trickle through. Weird and interesting shaped containers to show that water finds its own levels.

Sprays & Jets: syringes, washing-up bottles, water bottles, meat basters, plant sprays.

Capacity: small objects such as miniature metal jugs, dolls tea set, pipettes to drop water in. Containers to "fix" with tape/Bluetac™ to prevent water level from lowering.

Small Worlds In The Materials Tray

The materials tray can be used for contextual small world environments as well as a zone for exploring areas of the curriculum. The materials tray allows a more sensorial space than floor based play since polar bears can live in a place with water, rocks and pretend icebergs. Small world can also be provided alongside a construction zone. The stimulus for these experiences can come from a story, an interest or investigation.

These ideas are for small worlds that are placed in the materials tray or a container to make the most of water, leaves, potting compost and sand. Since the area is waterproof we can use real plants and textures that might otherwise become unmanageable.

Animals: Cloths that provide texture and colour, rocks, logs, bowls for water areas, small seedling trees. Play Mobil or other animals that can be angled.

Dinosaurs: Wood, stone, dry sand for desert habitat: plants (ferns) water and earth for swamp area. Dinosaur variety both in type and number so that the children can explore habitat and grouping such as herds.

Seashore: Sand, grit, water worn pebbles, stones for rock pools, seaweed (plastic or real), plastic wrapping paper that could represent water or use real water in the middle and sand on the outer rim.

Woodland: Wood logs, leaves, twigs, moss, real plants that are woodland based such as Primrose. Use of woodland puppets and models.

Opposites: use of materials and containers that enable children to explore dimensions such as up/down, in front and behind, inside and out within the play e.g. Black and white, opaque and transparent.

Houses and Homes: Sand, grit, gravel with a variety of tiny bricks, tubing to represent drains, twigs for trees, diggers, people.

Small World/Construction

Construction areas can be created in a variety of places from very large environments that can take place outside to small experiences in gravel trays on top of a bookcase.

- **The materials that are used in the construction area will affect the children that choose to go there or their level of engagement when they are playing**.

- **The organisation of the area should support children's exploration of different types of construction material.** Children need to have access to multiple construction sets that have a variety of techniques. Many apparently different construction sets actually use the same push-fit system.

- **The design of construction materials obviously influences the ultimate form they take, so therefore children should be allowed to choose appropriate materials and blend them together to make their structures.**
E.g. it is difficult to make a mosque if you only have Duplo™ because it has no curved bricks.

- **There should be progression in construction skills. These need to be identified to ensure there is enough challenge for children 3-8 years.** The skill level required to use some sets is far greater than others and the motivational context is often geared to a maturational level.

- **Construction areas work effectively when they have a defined area.** This can be created with a roofed area, fencing, bookcases or even a visual line on a carpet. For some children the organisation of a construction space into a role-play zone will enable them to engage more fully in the skills associated with construction.

- **The combination of characters and smaller resources will stimulate children to move beyond simple construction techniques.**

'Role play areas combined with construction'

'Self-check systems for clearing away'

A construction area should contain the following:

- Wooden bricks large and small
- Teifoc (earthenware bricks)
- Ventis (wooden log set)
- Duplo (brick shape)
- Meccano (metal set)
- Mobilo (wheels and hinges)
- Reo clic (towers and platforms)
- Driftwood for creative use
- Wooden sections of branches
- Fabric squares for roofs and floors
- Environmental print, such as building plans, diagrams and lists
- Visual stimulii such as photographs of building shape, local environments, close-ups of parts of buildings such as guttering, window sills, locks etc.
- Old hairdryers set to cold that can be used to test wind force.
- Small bags to put cargo into
- Tape measures
- Building plans
- Clipboard and paper for own plans
- Dry paint brushes to pretend to paint buildings and constructions
- Small materials such as gems and wooden shapes to embellish structures.

Outdoor play enables us to create construction areas on a larger scale. We do however have to be aware of the weather and the ability of the resources to withstand it. The following resources should be available through an outdoor box/resource base.

- Guttering
- Crates
- Real bricks such as fire bricks, mono blocks
- Sand, water and trowels to make cement
- Laminated building plans
- Building hats
- Tubing
- Walkie-talkies
- Larger tape measures
- Pacer wheel for long distances

The skills surrounding block play can be defined. Staff need to analyse equipment so they can see the potential of a resource that may at first appear to be very simple. Wooden blocks actually offer a huge amount more than some over-designed construction sets on the market this is because they are open-ended in their use. We limit children's creative learning through too many pre-designed and 'closed' construction sets.

Metallic sets such as Meccano provide progression from some of the simpler wooden construction sets. The introduction of structured cards adds a more challenging dimension to children's learning, in that they are following adult instructions and visualisation. Children can create their own prompt cards for the area with photographs of models they have made, diagrams they have drawn and visual images that they have taken .The aspects that children choose to photograph are often the detail that adults overlook, such as hinges, levers, door handles and catches.

'Interpreting diagrams to aid construction'

Wooden blocks can be shaped in a way that enables children to be creative and yet be stimulated in the thinking process. These blocks were used extensively by Froebel and are now seen in most early years environments. The creative blocks featured below are offering a more natural and sensorial resource for young children. The mathematical set has been created so that the blocks are created in centimetre lengths. Children can explore mathematical concepts through handling these materials. This mathematical aspect can be supported through the use of mark-making materials and centimetre squared paper, thus allowing children to create scale diagrams of their structures if they so desire. The possible lines of development (P.L.O.D.S.) are far reaching and often inter-connected.

Maths Blocks P.L.O.D.S:

- Height
- Diameter
- Stability with measure
- Cumulative addition
- Equivalence

'Exploration of measure through sensorial resources'

'Abstract shapes encourage creativity that can lead onto stories and artwork.'

P.L.O.D.S:

- Storying
- Storytelling
- Growing shapes
- Tessellations
- Shades of colour

'Real bricks - Teifoc can be used inside or out to explore structures. Photographic cues stimulate a variety of building styles.'

P.L.O.D.S:

- Stability of building types
- Bond/building styles
- Brick patterns
- Adhesion of mixtures/mortar
- Choice of material
- Effective foundation on stability

'A stimulating tree house is flexible with its addition of pulleys and levers to extend scientific exploration.'

P.L.O.D.S:

- Levers
- Pulleys for bucket and stairs
- Ratchet systems
- Manual dexterity of knot tying
- Measure of rope required

'Space to extend landscapes and ideas enables group socialisation.'

P.L.O.D.S:

- Perseverance
- Design
- Extensions of ideas
- Verbal reasoning skills

Creating a Cohesive Approach

The questions proposed at the start of this book suggested that the reader take some time to reflect on their personal belief about how young children learn. In conclusion I would like to share with you my experiences of how dedicated professionals are creating a cohesive approach, not just in Scotland but across the United Kingdom and the world.

Children are unique and we should treat them as we do the adults in our lives, this ensures that they are respected and given the opportunity to demonstrate their individuality. I listened in wonder to a song written by a young child in Australia sharing his questions of why and how things happen in the world. This individuality had been nurtured from an early age.

Children have their own way of learning, just as adults do. I watched a group of Icelandic teachers interact with a number of eight year olds to discover how each group was going to investigate the project rather than telling them how to do it.

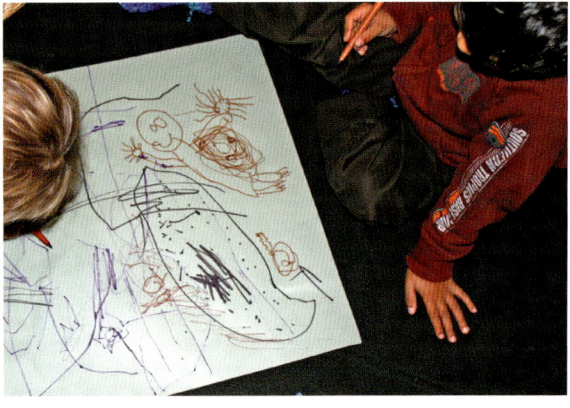

Children already have existing frameworks of understanding when they enter our more formalised education system. Listening to childrens voices is done naturally by some educators in all countries. In parts of Europe such as Italy, key centres have created their approach which is now inspiring others around the world to listen first and then teach.

Children need to be mobile to enquire and investigate. An attitude of curiosity drives the human race to push the boundaries of exploration. Attitudes develop very early in life and for many people are affected by our comfort zone. Children in our education system need to be active because that is their comfort zone, this then enables their brain to open up to learning.

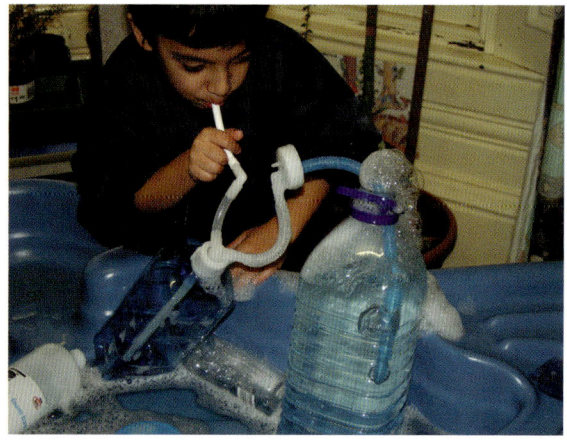

Children are thinkers and are remarkably good at reading situations. In order to conform to the classroom society I see children lose their drive and many accept seat based tasks. Just because children can sit still and conform does not mean it is the right thing to do. I have had conversations with six year old children who wistfully talk about learning outside but have picked up implicit messages from the adults around them that the adults don't feel comfortable in that space. Surely education should be about the needs of children!!

Children use communication and language to help them learn. Early learning environments that support oracy create children that can convey their thinking effectively. I was recently taught some Gaelic by a three year old in Glasgow, who delighted in using his knowledge to teach an adult.

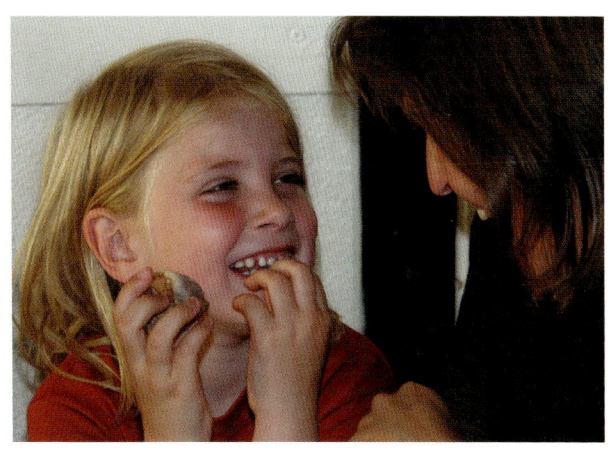

Children can be very independent from a very young age if the environment is set up to support this and there is an ethos of trust that movement can go hand in hand with learning.

Children are developing their self esteem. Their perception of themselves is formed early in life but goes on to affect lifelong learning and their emotional intelligence as adults. Human beings need to be valued and appreciated.

Governments around the world are trying to create a cohesive pathway of education. Communities within schools and centres are defining their interpretation. The practitioners are on a learning pathway themselves developing the methodology to implement policy, and the children that they care for are trying to find their pathway to lifelong learning. We need to create a cohesive pathway that puts children's rights and needs at the centre if we are to create an educational methodology to be proud of.

Appendix 1: Meeting the Challenges of Shared Spaces

Contextual Opportunities for the Open Area

Case Study

The examples that are provided here are based around the presentation of the 5-14 mathematics through play, and the extension of the other aspects of the 5-14 curriculum in an integrated planner.

The system was set up to develop play across two classes of P1 to P3 with possible inclusion of composite classes in the future. The area is accessible to all the classes within a shared open area. The planning overview was designed to ensure that there were common threads running through the play area that could be picked up by each class during their timetabled time. On average this was 3 x 1 hour sessions a week. The area was available every morning to Primary 1 for maths and language experiences.

In this particular school the 5-14 is divided into themes that ensure balance and breadth across the school. The frameworks are flexible to encourage teachers to respond to children's interest. The example below shows the Environmental studies for 2002/3.

Primary 1 5 years	My School	Caring & Sharing (Health)	My School (Tech)	Myself (S.S.)
Primary 1/2 5 - 6 years (Science)	People Who Help Us (S.S.)	The Seasons (Tech)	Weather (S.S., Weather)	Seasonal Needs
Primary 2 6 years	Caring for Me (S.S.)	Toys (Tech)	Comparative Studies (S.S.)	Games and Leisure (S.S.)
Primary 3 7 years	Village Study (S.S.)	Buildings in the Village	Grand-parents (S.S.)	A Health Environment
Primary 3/4 7 - 8 years	Town Study/ enterprise	Shops and Shopping	Construction Project (Tech)	The Senses (S.C.)

Using this as the framework the following outline was created that enabled the same open area to be used by 6 classes and possibly 8. This allowed similar resources to be used by the groups, but with a different learning intention or context so that there was some relevance to the children visiting the area.

Overview of the open area with possible tasks linked to aspects of Environmental Studies/RME/Mathematics/English Language/Expressive Arts.

This is only a framework around the existing paths laid out for breadth and balance throughout 5-14. It is open to change as long as the opportunities link across the use of the open area for all classes in Primary 1 through to Primary 3

Theme running through the shared open area is identified in italics. Linked displays celebrating the process of exploration and play, and talking and thinking books are integral to the approach and provide valuable feedback for assessment and monitoring. Additional materials and a programme of independent tasks were organised and made available.

Primary 1	My School *Textures and materials leading to Maps and mapping 3d models of the school*	Caring and Sharing (gifts) *Exploration of 3d shape leading to creation of gift and box* *RME- Baptism gift*	My School (Tech) *Electricity leading to Lights and lighting*	Myself *Growing and the effect on plants and animals.*
P1/2	People Who Help Us *Textures and materials Leading to exploration of types of fabrics used in uniforms such as reflexite etc.*	The Seasons *Design and creation of shelters and home for wildlife*	Weather *Natural forms of light such as rainbows. Exploration of colour mixing and splitting light.*	Seasonal Needs *Seasonal variation in plants and the cycle of the seasons*
P2	Caring for me *Textures and materials Leading to creating own objects for the dentist..toothpaste/ new brush*	Toys *Design and Creation of Robot from Junk*	Comparative Sudy (Gambia) *Alternative forms of energy, wind power, dynamo torches etc.*	Games and Leisure *Gardens... old and new designs. Garden design for specific need.*
P3	Village Study *Textures and materials leading to textural maps/ surfaces of village*	Buildings in Village *Design and creation of buildings from 3d shapes*	Grandparents *Lighting in our grandparents day.* *RME Haanukah lights.*	Healthy Environment *Pollution and the effect on plant life*
P3/4	Town Study (Enterprise) *As above or Enterprise project to design an object where texture is important.*	Shops and Shopping *Design and creation of storage and packaging for food stuffs e.g new egg box, carrier bag*	Construction Project *Design and construction of a lamp with simple wiring circuit and shade.*	The Senses *Variety of smells in nature*

The resourcing and setting up of the area was therefore spread across all the year groups. Common threads and individual class responses were monitored though the talking and thinking books. Primary 2 and 3 were given individual books and encouraged to use strategies such as mind maps, diagrams etc to record their discoveries. Primary 1 gave oral feedback/group talking and thinking books.

Children working in level A (towards B) in Mathematics from any class were given the opportunity to access the concepts through a materials tray, water, discovery den, malleable materials, (role play available in each room as a role play bag). The resources were placed in to separate wallets and labelled, stored and accessed through nearby cupboards. This system allowed smaller practical experiences to take place in the classroom bays as table top activities.

Case Study – New Friends

A group of 30 five year olds were involved in meeting people from the community to raise their awareness of disability and the effect it has on day to day living. The experience of filling in a two dimensional workbook about daily visitors had some elements that showed that children enjoyed meeting people, however the staff felt that the experience had more potential for learning.

The whole class came together to hear the overview of the session, to put the activity / experience into a context that had some relevance to them.

The children were invited to sign up to the Talking and Thinking Floorbook and in so doing they were encouraged to share a highlight from the week. The base line supported the adult in that the amount of knowledge the children had stretched out far beyond the capacity of the booklet. The challenge was to share the thinking and enable each child to share their perspective on a subject that many adults struggle to discuss.

A series of experiences were set up to physically engage the whole class. Children could choose their challenge and were told at the start of the session that the overall objective was 'to be able to talk to the adults to reflect on the challenge' the success criteria was created by the children to be to talk about 2 different challenges and talk about the tricky bits! The adult structure was to consider the learning behind the opportunities and to consider possible lines of development.

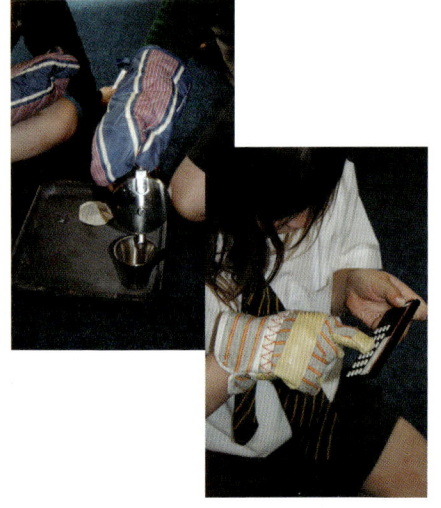

- Hinge and lock mechanisms to undo whilst wearing a blindfold (life skills and no vision).

- Do up a pair of shoes whilst wearing gloves (life skill of increasing challenge and reduced dexterity).

- Make a pot of tea with real teabags (and cold water) whilst wearing oven gloves. (food / drink handling with reduced dexterity).

- Calculate a simple sum using a calculator and garden gloves (mental acuity and physical challenge).

- Listen to a story tape with ear defenders on (auditory challenge).

The Talking and Thinking tree was set up with paper leaves around it and on the table children were encouraged to handle models of equipment such as wheelchairs, crutches, shaped cutlery etc and models of people to stimulate talk. The ideas were recorded on the leaves. The type of comments were 'Sophie's wheelchair is called squiggles.', 'Duncan uses a communication board to speak – has lots of colours.', 'Peter fell off his motorbike, he was going fast.', 'Alison had glasses.', 'She calls her daddy even when she doesn't need him!' The children then drew their own trees into the Floorbook and glued their leaves onto the trees.

The third group were based on the carpet area and had direct support from the adult to write into the Talking and Thinking Floorbook to discuss and record their perceptions of the week. Children made detailed drawings/ diagrams of a modern wheelchair, crutches and funky resources such as drinking cups and remote control tools. They spoke about the personality of the people and how some had been born with 'bits not working' and others had incurred injuries through accidents.

The groups came to the mat with their thinking on separate leaves to organise and reflect on some of their ideas. The adult asked them to consider what we now know about the way people live their lives, 'our new friends' was written by the adult as the central point. The challenge was offered of how our ideas could then be sorted. Children looked at their own ideas on the leaves and the group came forward with ideas which were written onto yellow strips of paper.

The ideas given were:
people, equipment they use, their stories, adult added understanding. The equipment line then subdivided into wheelchair, crutches, glasses etc. At this point the group put down their ideas at the place on the map where they felt it should go. The photographs show the process of thinking as children moved leaves (ideas) around so that they were happy with the result.

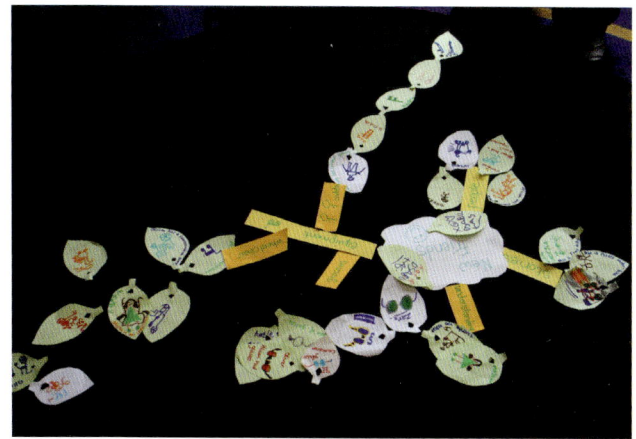

Learning Pathways   77

The area that had most awareness and discussion was around the tools required and their design. One child had remembered a visitor who had asked her mum for a new drinking cup. This became the focus for the next opportunity for learning and required phone calls and conversations with the little girl to find out what she needed and how she could hold it.

P.L.O.D.s

- Exploration into design and function generally in school
- Ergonomics and ease of use
- Properties of materials for cups
- Design elements of colour, line and pattern
- The construction of spouts and flow rates through different holes
- Reflection on personal design to meet need such as a picnic cup for outdoor picnics

This transferred to the areas in the classroom.

The Discovery Den

Outcome: Properties of materials for cups.
Children will be able to sort china, pottery, plastic, wood for a variety of criteria.

Materials Tray

Outcome: The construction of spouts and flow rates through different holes.
Children will be able to talk about the choice of the hole diameter for ease of use.

Malleable Area

Outcome: Ergonomics and ease of use.
Children will explain their choice of handle/ grip for the mug.

Outdoor Play

Outcome: The application of design for a new product.
Children will make comparisons and experiment with various liquids.

Role Play

Outcome: An awareness of the variety of cups available and the exploration of colour line and texture.
Children will be aware of the range of cups and their uses in the role play scenarios.

Bibliography

Bennett, Neville. (1976) Teaching Styles and Pupil Progress, Open Books, London

Blatchford, P. (1982) The First Transition; Home to Pre- School. NFER nelson

Bruner, Jerome. (1960) The Process of Education

Burke, Pat and Stephen Garger (1986) Marching to Different Drummers ASCD. USA

Caswell, Chris (1993) Body Language for Competent Teachers, Routledge, London.

Cleave, S. (1982) *And so to school.* Research project. NFER Nelson

Curtis, A. (1991) A Curriculum for the pre-school child NFER, Nelson

Jensen, Eric. (1995) Superteaching, Turning point Publishing, California

David, T. (1990) Under Five - Under Educated. Open University Press

Fabien. Dr.H. (2002) *Contextualised Learning for 5-8 year olds.* Learning and Teaching Scotland

Forman & Cadzean (1985)

Fisher, J. (1996) *Starting from the Child* Open University Press

Fisher, Robert. (1995) Teaching children to Learn, Stanley Thornes, Cheltenham

Goleman, Daniel. (1996) Emotional Intelligence, Bloomsbury, London

Hargreaves, David. (1975) Interpersonal Relations and Education, Routledge and Kegan, Paul. London.

Holmann, M. et al (1979) Young children in action High Scope Press

Hurst, V. (1991) Planning for Early Learning .Paul Chapman

HMI (1989) Effective Primary Schools

HMIE (2007) Curriculum for Excellence

Kyriacou, Chris. (1986) Effective teaching in Schools. Blackwell, London

McGettrick, Bart (1995). Ensuring Progression in Learning . Glasgow

Moyles, J. (1991) Play as a Learning Process in your Classroom, MGP

Nias, J. (1989) Primary Teachers Talking

Scottish CCC (1995) The Heart of the Matter. Scottish Consultative Council for Curriculum, Dundee.

Scottish Executive Education Department (2001) *Early Intervention* interchange 71 Published by same.

SCRE. (1995) Taking a closer look at Science

SOED (1993) Structure and Balance of the 5-14 curriculum

SOED (1994) Education of children under five in Scotland, HMI

Sylvester. Robert (1994) How Emotions Affect Learning Educational Leadership ASCD. USA

Smith, A (1999) The Alps Approach Network Education Press. Ltd

Vygotsky (1978) Mind and Society. Harvard University Press

Warden, Claire. (1999) Outdoor Play. Mindstretchers

Warden, Claire. (2001) Dramatic Play. Mindstretchers

Warden, Claire. (2005) Potential of a Puddle. Mindstretchers

Warden, Claire. (2006) Talking & Thinking Floorbooks. Mindstretchers